SALONOVATIONS' GUIDE TO BECOMING A FINANCIALLY SOLVENT SALON

NOTICE TO THE READER

Cover Design by: D. Dupras
Photographs Courtesy: Ann Freehill

Milady Staff:

Publisher: Catherine Frangie
Acquisitions Editor: Marlene McHugh Pratt
Production Manager: Brian Yacur
Project Development Editor: Laura Miller
Project Editor: Annette Downs Danaher
Art/Design Production Coordinator: Suzanne McCarron

Copyright © 1996
Milady Publishing Company
(a division of Delmar Publishers)

Printed in the United States of America
Printed and distributed simultaneously in Canada

For more information, contact:
    SalonOvations
    Milady Publishing Company
    3 Columbia Circle, P.O. Box 12519
    Albany, New York 12212-2519

1 2 3 4 5 6 7 8 9 10 XXX 01 00 99 98 97 96

LIBRARY OF CONGRESS CATALOGING-IN-PUBLICATION DATA

Edgerton, Leslie.
    SalonOvations' guide to becoming a financially solvent salon/by Leslie Edgerton and Glen R. Allie.
        p. cm.
    Includes index.
    ISBN 1-56253-211-1
    1. Beauty Shops—Management. I. Allie, Glen R.
TT965.E324 1996
646.7'2'068—dc20   95-16204
                                                                          CIP

SALONOVATIONS' GUIDE TO BECOMING A FINANCIALLY SOLVENT SALON

by

Leslie Edgerton
and
Glen R. Allie, C.P.A.

Milady Publishing Company
(a division of Delmar Publishers)
3 Columbia Circle, Box 12519
Albany, New York 12212-2519

Delmar Publishers' Online Services
To access Delmar on the World Wide Web, point your browser to:
http://www.delmar.com/delmar.html
To access through Gopher: **gopher://gopher.delmar.com**
(Delmar Online is part of "thomson.com," an Internet site with information on more
than 30 publishers of the International Thomson Publishing organization.)
For information on our products and services:
email: **info@delmar.com**
or call **800-347-7707**

Table of Contents

Acknowledgments

Many people are involved in the successful production of a book and richly deserve the gratitude of not only the authors, but of those readers who come away with something of value. We owe large debts to a number of people. Ann Freehill comes to mind first, our photographer who worked "under the gun" within a very limited time frame and produced the kind of professional work she is noted for. Catherine Frangie and Annette Danaher, our editors, both deserve a lengthy vacation for all the patience and guidance they provided during the course of this writing, as does Laura Miller our Project Development Editor. There are many other editors who deserve kudos. Special thanks go to Lowell Williams, CLU, of Schrader & Associates, who provided in-depth insurance expertise and to Bob Parker of Navistar, who was our computer guru.

Both of us owe a great deal to our wives, Joyce and Mary, for their input and assistance, not only with this book, but in life as we know it.

A special thank-you to the following individuals who devoted their time and expertise to the review of this manuscript:

Don Osborne, Costa Mesa, CA
Marilyn Deglomine, Altamonte Springs, FL
Victoria Harper, Kokomo, IN
Cynthia Schultz, Cuyahoga Falls, OH

About the Authors

Accountant Glen R. Allie, C.P.A. has practiced accounting for sixteen years and is the Vice-President of Del Principe and Allie, C.P.A.'s, P.C. Married to Joyce, father of Tanya and Allison, he graduated from St. Joseph's College in Rensselaer, Indiana in 1978. He is a member of the American Institute of C.P.A.'s and the Indiana C.P.A. Society, and is certified in Educational Achievement and Personal Financial Planning.

Salon owner Leslie Edgerton is a sixteen-time winner of state hairstyling championships and trophies in Indiana, Illinois and Michigan. A successful hairstylist and designer for twenty-eight years, Edgerton has also been a platform artist for Clairol. He currently writes a quarterly column on retailing for *Nails Magazine*, and has been a contributing editor to *Hair and Beauty News*; has written numerous articles for such publications as *Brides, Bridal Trends*, and *National Beauty School Journal*; and has had technicals and photos of his work in such magazines as *Touts, Dixie Magazine*, and *Gambit*. He was a contributing author to Milady's *Standard Textbook of Cosmetology* and is the author of *You and Your Clients: Milady's Human Relations for Cosmetology* and *Managing Your Business: Milady's Guide to the Salon*.

Edgerton has also been featured on the television show "PM Magazine" and on Cox Cable in an in-depth interview with Paul Cimino. A graduate with honors of Indiana University, he is presently working toward his MFA in Writing at Vermont College. Along with nonfiction, Edgerton also writes novels and short literary fiction. He has had many short stories published in literary magazines and anthologies and won a national award for his novel *Spatterdashers*, published by The University of North Texas Press, which is forthcoming. He and his wife, Mary, own and operate Bold Strokes Hair Designers in Ft. Wayne, Indiana. They have a son,

Michael Bud, and Edgerton has two daughters, Britney and Sienna from a previous marriage.

About The Photographer

Ann Freehill's first exposure to photography came at the age of sixteen when she took a summer school class in photography. It was love at first sight. That class opened a whole new world to her. Nearly thirty years later the love is still there. Over the years, Ann has studied various forms of her art at Indiana-Purdue University at Ft. Wayne and St. Francis College. Her work has been exhibited at Artlink, the Allen County Public Library, the Weatherhead Gallery, and the Wassenberg Art Center in Van Wert, Ohio. Currently, Ann resides in Fort Wayne, Indiana, with her husband, two daughters and three cats.

Dedication

To the many thousands of talented, hard-working hairstylists who have given beauty to the world; to our wives and children, who sacrificed so that this book might get written; to the editors and others who worked to produce a quality book; to the professionals who "crunch the numbers" that allows us to run salons at a profit; to all these and many more unnamed and deserving individuals, Glen and I dedicate this guide, in hopes that not only financially but spiritually, your lives will be enriched. In particular, I would like to dedicate this effort to my mother, Dorothy Edgerton, who has always been my moral beacon and shining example of what can be accomplished through faith and principle.

Preface

Hairstylists have traditionally operated their businesses with one hand tied behind their backs.

While many other businesses of all sizes have gurus to assist and guide them in making sound financial business decisions, those of us in the salon industry have mostly lacked professional "number crunchers" and financial whizzes to help us arrive at sound business decisions.

Such questions as *Should we retool?*, *Should we reduce (or add) personnel?*, or *Is it feasible to bring out a new product?* are all concerns that are routinely studied and analyzed either by in-company financial professionals or by retaining highly-paid and qualified consultants, or both. The president of General Motors doesn't just wake up one fine morning and decree that the automaker is going to begin manufacturing a new line of sedans. There are formulas that are used to test the projected profitability, studies to determine if there is a sufficient market to buy a new car, and a host of other considerations to be calculated, perused and analyzed, sometimes to death.

The point is, most successful businesses don't operate "from the hip pocket"—there is a lot of intelligent thought that goes into the process before monetary decisions are reached.

In our industry, this is not often the case. For one thing, our salons aren't ordinarily large enough concerns to be able to afford the kind of professional assistance necessary to conduct the sophisticated studies needed to put our financial decisions on a sounder business footing. We tend to operate under the principle of "educated guesses." The downside to this is that many times we haven't yet acquired the business or financial acumen necessary to arrive at the best decisions, and perhaps aren't even aware of other options that may be more suitable.

That is the purpose of this book.

This text is designed to put at your fingertips the kinds of tools other businesses take for granted in their decision-making processes. Together with the expertise of Certified Public Accountant, Glen Allie, we have compiled formulas and given you the logical business factors specifically designed to assist salons in arriving at practical, sensible, sound decisions that will add to the profitability of your bottom line. This book, we believe, is long overdue for our industry, and is especially critical now, with the massive changes in our industry and the economy in general currently underway.

Over the past few years, tumultuous shifts in the political climate, which greatly affect the economic world we exist in, indicate that great change is forthcoming. The salon owner who is fully prepared for these sweeping winds of transformation will be better equipped to survive and even prosper. In industry after industry, downsizing, mergers, acquisitions, and other related activities are resulting in more and more larger businesses and fewer individual firms.

Look at what's happened in manufacturing, publishing, farming, food service, transportation...in short, virtually all business activities are increasingly being conducted by fewer and fewer companies. The small operator, a definition most in our industry fall under, is increasingly being forced to compete with bigger and better-equipped companies, companies with infinite resources. Someone predicted (only half-jokingly) that in a dozen years, two companies would own everything...and that the larger of those two would be out secretly buying up the stock of the other!

Thirty years ago, there were "mom and pop" grocery stores everywhere. Now, a handful of giant chains owns most of the food outlets where we shop. At one time, there were ice cream shops with as many different names as there were owners—try to locate an independent that's not allied with a national franchise within walking distance of your house or apartment! The list goes on and on. Family-owned breweries, regional automakers, small, family farms and ranches are disappearing rapidly; the list is virtually endless and includes almost any service or product one can name.

That is not to say that small business cannot survive and prosper, but it is imperative that they learn all they can of the business principles necessary to compete with the larger operators with their vast resources. Those who are ill-prepared will find it increasingly difficult to maintain their businesses in the black and may even be forced to close their doors. We are not trying to paint a picture of doom and gloom, only a realistic one in which all the signs point to tough times ahead for those salon owners who do not adhere to and practice good judgment in their financial dealings. The days of establishing and maintaining a profitable salon business strictly on the strength of artistic talent are largely gone. Business acumen is no longer a luxury that will merely increase an already healthy net gain; it is an absolute necessity, crucial to basic survival.

Our aim is that this book will become a valuable weapon in your business arsenal, and that you continue to learn as much as you can about the world of business in general and the salon business in particular, for knowledge is surely the key to prosperity.

Gather as much information as you possibly can, and you will not only maintain a steady cash flow, but you will leap ahead of those who don't possess the tools you have gained. Read texts such as this, go to seminars, and learn, learn, learn! Travel outside the relatively narrow boundaries of salons and styling and seek as much information as you can about business in general and economics as a whole. The pursuit and acquisition of knowledge is a heady, exciting thing, and allows one not only to get ahead in the business of hairstyling but in the business of life itself.

Keep in mind that while the concept of "rugged individualism" is a time-honored and revered American tradition, when carried to the extreme, it, like all principles, brings with it a potential danger. It must be tempered with a bit of common sense. Certainly, small business owners are the epitome of such admirable moralities, but it is not against the spirit of capitalistic endeavor to seek out and utilize the knowledge of others in the creation of your slice of the American dream. As C. L. Smith pointed out, "Show me a man who has become a success, and I'll show you a man who had help getting there." Whatever success we have ourselves personally enjoyed in our own salon business can be directly traced to our own efforts, to be sure, but credit must also go to many others who have pointed out the way to us and helped us find the best paths to travel.

The best of luck to you in your quest for excellence!

CHAPTER ONE

Preparing and Using a Budget

Just as one wouldn't dream of beginning a long motor trip to far-away and new places without a road map, a salon owner shouldn't consider embarking on the journey her salon will be taking into the future without a proper guide. The road map for that kind of excursion is the salon budget.

Providing for your expenses and allocating your resources is the *job* of a budget. The *value* of a budget is that it gives you a tool to more accurately forecast the economic future of your salon. No business yet exists that can predict exactly what the future will bring, but a budget gets you much closer to a more precise prognosis. Budgets can help you make better decisions on such matters as when to hire and fire, when to expand or add services or products, where costs can be reduced, and many other factors that impact the bottom line.

And make no mistake—a profitable bottom line is the primary requirement of any salon that intends to stay in business. Without a profit, nothing else will occur—the business will cease to exist. Everything must be subject to this goal or any other goals will be unmet.

A good accounting system is essential to the success of your business. It is the foundation to decisions that will be made in the direction your business should take. It provides a basis with which to achieve goals and to help establish priorities. A good accounting system makes you "accountable" for your actions or lack thereof.

Also, a good accounting system is the best defense in the case of an Internal Revenue Service audit. The burden of proof for deductions and the reporting of income is the responsibility of the taxpayer.

A good accounting system enables the user to categorize cash inflows and outflows for the determination of net income or loss. It provides the basis for setting goals in the determination of future

A good accounting system is the best defense in an IRS audit.

BIG GAME
IRS VS
SERENDIPITY SALON

The best defense for business is an accounting system.

expenses (i.e., budget), and provides a history of the business' activity to calculate formulas discussed in this book.

Here's where a budget comes in and flexes its muscle. It is a road map for the future of your business. Gross sales and services drive the business' profits, however, a control of expenses can add great benefits to the bottom line. A budget is not designed to cut expenses or reduce flexibility in spending money, rather, a budget is a method by which you can determine a level of spending to match the current income that is being produced. It is a tool by which to measure the achievement or nonachievement of the goals you have established for your salon.

Gross income should be categorized to accounts describing the way in which inflows are received. Examples would include Service Income versus Retail Sales by department (i.e., Hair Products, Nail Products). Cost of Sales should accompany each retail sales account.

The sample income and cost of sales section would appear as follows:

GROSS SALES AND SERVICE:

Sales:

    Sales—Hair Products Direct

    Sales—Nail Products

    Sales—Other

        Total Sales

Services:

    Service Income—Haircuts

    Service Income—Perms

    Service Income—Other

        Total Service Income

        Total Gross Income

Expenses should be listed in as much detail as can be controlled. With the aid of computer programs, this task is a lot easier than it was many years ago.

Expenses that are not controllable can be summarized into broad categories. However, you will soon find that you will want to provide as much detail in your expense categories to allow yourself the ability to review the account activity without a lot of hassle. Therefore, a suggestion is that the expense accounts provide as much detail as possible with groupings used to report totals.

Here is an example. Your telephone bill can be divided into several categories. Local, Long Distance, Cellular, Business Use of Home Phone, and Advertising. If you recorded the telephone bill to a single account, the ability to monitor the listed breakdowns would be impossible unless you spent hours dividing the numbers at analysis time. If, however, you record the expense breakdown at the time the expense was recorded in the accounting records, what a savings of time and what a wealth of knowledge you now possess.

If you were ready to switch long distance carriers, and needed to know "How much did I spend on long distance phone calls?", the answer would be readily available. If you needed to know if more phone lines in the salon would accommodate your clientele, the answer would be there.

More importantly, if you are to determine if your goals are being met in spending, what better way to arrive at this information than to have this data available? It may appear tedious at first, but once you have established your categories and get in the habit of entering them promptly, the benefits you will gain will make the time well spent.

Many computer programs allow you the ability to enter budgets for your expense categories and provide a plethora of reports to help begin to analyze the differences between your *budgeted* income and expenses and the *actual* income and expenses. Your accountant can provide a great deal of information on this topic and should assist you in establishing your budget. However, it is up to *you* to get the job done!

The following accounts could be used in categorizing income and expenses. The need is to "match" certain revenues and cost of sales. For example, if you are monitoring the sale of retail items, there should exist a corresponding cost of sales account so that the owner can calculate gross margins. In addition, the salon owner can establish departments for the salon, to incorporate specific, individual segments that are characteristic of your own enterprise.

Total Gross Income (see above)

Less Cost of Sales (by department)
- Beginning Inventory
- Purchases
- (Ending Inventory)

Equals Gross Margin

Less Labor
- Wages
- Employee Benefits
- Payroll Tax Expense

Less Operating Supplies—Direct

Equals Gross Profit

Less Operating Expenses
- Selling Expenses
- Occupancy Costs
- Administrative Expenses

Equals Net Income (Loss)

Other segments of your budget should be handled in the same fashion. As each salon operation is different, you should consult with your accountant in setting up your own budget. It is better to consult with a professional than to try to utilize some sort of "boiler-plate" template. Sitting down together and mapping out your goals will result in an instrument that will aid greatly in maximizing your efforts and point out future possibilities. Remember that a budget is a flexible, *living* instrument, that should be reviewed and amended as time goes on and a history gradually develops.

CHAPTER TWO

Staff Compensation and Benefits

Traditionally, most salons have utilized a commission scheme to compensate their stylists for their labors, while a few have paid a salary or a combination of both. In the past, benefits have been ignored, largely because most salons have felt they were unaffordable. Other staffers, such as receptionists, have usually been salaried, either at a weekly, fixed rate, or based on an hourly rate.

As Bob Dylan croons in a once-famous song, "...the times, they are a'changin'."

The economics of today dictates that salon owners can no longer realistically disregard benefit packages if they wish to attract quality personnel who increasingly insist upon them. Commission rates of payment, if not being abolished, are being drastically changed from what they were even a few short years ago. This change is a necessity if the salon expects to remain financially healthy.

Back when I began in the business, some twenty-five years ago, it was common to pay the stylist 70–75% of what they brought in, and I was even paid at the rate of 85% by one salon! Today, salons on a commission schedule only routinely offer 40–50%. It is not unusual to see salons paying designers 30–35% and in some instances, even lower rates, although salons paying these lower rates usually provide a benefits package as well.

Since commissions have been the primary compensation scheme for so long in our business, it is difficult to change the mind-set of many owners and employees. It isn't easy to entertain thoughts of a different compensation arrangement, even though the handwriting may be on the wall for the demise, or at least the drastic restructuring, of this system. If a compensation system, no matter how ingrained in tradition, becomes nonproductive to the salon, it will by necessity evolve into something more appropriate

Provide a pay scale equitable to both you and the employee.

to good business practices, and that is what we have seen happening in the last decade.

The first requirement for whatever compensation package you incorporate into your salon is that whatever is paid out does not eliminate profits. By the same measure, you need to arrive at an equitable pay scale that is fair to both you and your employees. If your pay arrangement guarantees a profit on paper, but you cannot find employees to work for that arrangement, then it doesn't much matter how you pay!

On the other hand, *providing jobs for stylists is not the primary business of a salon. Returning a profit, is.* A salon can survive and even thrive without any employees other than the owner, but no salon can survive very long if a profit margin is not maintained.

One very important component of a salary scheme is the tax/burden rate. The tax/burden rate is made up of the following minimum items:

- FICA

- State Unemployment

- Federal Unemployment

- Workers' Compensation Insurance

Each state has its own unemployment and workers' compensation rates, but for purposes of example, we will use the states of Indiana and Ohio.

TAX/BURDEN RATES*		
	Indiana Technical	Ohio Technical
FICA	7.6500%	7.6500%
State Unemployment	2.7000%	3.000%
Federal Unemployment	0.8000%	0.8000%
Workers' Compensation Insurance	0.2709%	0.8646%
Total Burden Rate	11.4209%	12.3146%

*The current rates at the time of this writing.

This means that you, as an employer in either of these two states, will have to pay this percentage of the employee's salary in various taxes. An Indiana owner, for instance, will pay out $11.43 ($100.00 × 11.4209%) for every $100.00 in wages.

Here's a personal story coauthor Edgerton has to tell about how the wrong compensation scheme can harm a salon:

Years ago, I started up a salon in a medium-sized city and the salon was an instant success. Within a few short months, I was not only booked solid, but six weeks ahead, and at prices that were double the next-highest-priced salon in town. Deciding I needed to expand, I hired a stylist and agreed to pay him at the standard rate of the time, which was 70%. He brought absolutely no clientele with him, as the clients he had been servicing wouldn't pay our rates (to him) which were more than double what he had been charging in his old salon. But that was all right—he achieved a full booking immediately, solely on my overflow which I recommended to him.

My gross income went up accordingly, but a funny thing happened. Whereas before this hire, I had been putting a lot of money into savings and other investment vehicles, all of a sudden, I found the flow of disposable income had shrunk considerably. Puzzled, I went to my accountant to find out why. "You are losing seventy cents every time he performs a haircut, by paying him at 70%," my accountant told me. The percentage I was paying him was too high for the expenses incurred. When I informed him I was going to have to cut his percentage and even showed him the figures to back this up, he quit to open his own shop. With the reduced percentage he would still have earned more than twice what he ever had before, though the percentage I offered was not even what it *should* have been—it

Pay your stylists commission rates that bring a reasonable profit to the salon.

represented the break-even point. I felt bad about bringing him on board at one figure and then lowering him, so I decided to not lower it to a percentage that would have returned a profit for the salon—a mistake he rectified by quitting.

The point is, I made a mistake when I hired him by paying him the same percentage commonly offered at the time, which probably accounted for the great number of salons that closed their doors in the early 1970s.

Don't make the mistake, if you use commissions, of blindly following the pack. The "pack" may not be in business long, or if they are, they may not earn a reasonable profit.

The cost-volume-profit relationships, important in all business decisions, also impact how you should pay your employees. The interrelationships of all the affecting factors must be studied. An analysis must be made to determine how the services and goods are to be priced, which will allow you to compensate employees according to the pay scheme you employ. You must also determine, as realistically as possible, what will happen in the market. After you have figured in these factors and arrived at the costs to the salon of a service and/or product (including the staffer's salary and benefits), then you need to add the profit margin you desire. A reasonable profit margin is usually between 15 and 20% above all costs.

A salon's compensation policy should be designed to accomplish three primary objectives. It needs to attract qualified staff, retain employees, and recognize and reward the performance of high-quality work. The costs of a service business can be divided into three segments. They are:

1. Labor
2. Overhead
3. Owner Profit

The rule of thumb to determine the amount you should charge for an employee's time is 3 to 3.5 times the employee's labor cost. Direct labor cost includes paid benefits and working condition fringes. Therefore, if an employee's cost is $100, the service should be charged at $300 to $350.

FORMULA

Service Value	= SV
Cost of Labor	= L
Multiple	= 3.5
Direct Labor Cost	= $100

SOLUTION:

$$SV = L \times M$$
$$SV = \$100 \times 3.5$$
$$SV = \$350$$

The formula could be used in the inverse to determine labor cost where:

$$SV = L \times M$$
$$L = SV/M$$

SOLUTION:

$$L = SV/M$$
$$L = \$350/3.5$$
$$L = \$100$$

If your costs to provide the service are more or less than one-third of the total service, adjustments can be made to decrease or increase the percentage of compensation.

Fringe benefits have become an important part of an employee's overall compensation. Benefits must be clearly communicated as to the value derived by the employee if they are to be a meaningful part of an employee's overall compensation.

The following is a list of major benefits offered by service businesses:

Paid Vacation. Base this benefit on length of service. For example, one week after one year of service (hiring date).

Paid Holidays. Most businesses pay for six holidays in a natural business year: New Year's Day, Memorial Day, Independence Day, Labor Day, Thanksgiving and Christmas.

A benefit more and more businesses are providing for—day care services.

Sick Leave. Sick leave allowances exist in some businesses. It is the opinion of the authors that sick leave encourages absenteeism and therefore is not encouraged as a fringe benefit.

Dependent Day Care Services. An employee who receives dependent care assistance payments provided under an employer's written nondiscriminatory plan generally may exclude such payments from gross income. However, the exclusion is subject to an earned income limitation. The employee should seek professional advice as to the excludable portion. (An employer considering offering this benefit should consult with an accountant or other professional familiar with his or her business for advice as to whether or not this is feasible and how it should be implemented.)

Group Insurance. As of this writing, the Health Care Bill is pending in Congress. This could have a dramatic effect on employer and employee costs. Therefore, this discussion will be limited to the programs currently available. Group insurance costs can be paid either partially or fully by the employer. Added dependent coverage is sometimes made available on the payment of an extra insured.

Pension and Profit-Sharing Retirement Plans. In the past, many employees wanted to have employers "pay into" an employee's retirement plan. Times have changed. With the demands on an employee's personal finances, many employees would rather have increased current benefits than benefits that can be received "down the road." The employees realize that the retirement contribution has a cost to the employer and therefore represents a part of their total compensation package. They are willing to forego the retirement plan contribution (future dollars) for the money today. In addition, the contribution to a retirement plan is mandatory year after year. The Internal Revenue Service requires the filing of annual forms to account for the activity of the plan. It is our opinion that the situation needs to be evaluated individually to determine if there exists a benefit to the owner. If not, an employee bonus would be more appropriate from which they could fund their own retirement.

Reimbursement for Business Expenses. Reimbursements can be made for expenses incurred by the employee that benefit the business. These include meals and entertainment, and travel expenses in attending business meetings on behalf of the company. Meals and entertainment must be incurred in the normal course of business and must have documentation. The documentation must include *who* was present, *what* was discussed, *where* the meeting took place, *when* the meeting took place, and *how much* was charged. In 1994, only 50% of the meal will be deductible. The Internal Revenue Service has attacked this area of the law for many years, and therefore documentation of the event along with substantiating how this enhances your business is a necessity.

Reimbursement for Professional Expenses. Businesses reimburse part or all of the cost for attending professional seminars and conferences. This may include the cost of the event, meals, hotel, and travel. In 1994, travel reimbursements are $.29 per mile.

Again, many, if not most, of these benefits are new to salon owners, even though they have been part of compensation packages by other service businesses. As the labor pool becomes more sophisticated about such things, salons not offering comparable benefits may find themselves attracting fewer quality employees. Given a choice, why would a young person invest considerable time and money in studying for a profession (cosmetology) that offers little or no benefits and pays at a rate too low to purchase her own benefits, along with a livable wage? Especially, when for the same investment, training could be obtained for a field in which both the benefit package and wage are significantly better? When you look around at what has happened to the salon business in the past two or three decades, this is exactly what has transpired.

This is a problem that is occurring more and more frequently, and is a symptom of salon management clinging to old compensation schemes that no longer are feasible in today's economic climate. The way it is today, talented and qualified hairstylists increasingly see salon ownership as the only avenue to a decent wage and benefits package, and as soon as many are able, they quit the salon to open their own. If a more equitable scheme of compensation were implemented, this type of turnover (and subsequent competition) would significantly decrease.

Part of the problem is the reluctance of many owners to raise the price of services in order to provide sufficient wages and benefits (as well as a fair profit to the owner). It is no easy decision to raise fees, but in many cases not to do so spells the ultimate demise of the business. If a salon doesn't charge enough to attract quality employees, this will have a direct effect upon the amount of business the salon will achieve. Eventually, no matter what kind of "bargain" is offered consumers, the perception will be of an inferior product and service sales will begin to suffer, perhaps to the point where the business has to be closed. There is a definite "ripple effect" at work in such instances. Situations such as this need to be looked at closely, in partnership with a qualified professional, and changes made to make the salon healthy again.

Increased benefits and/or salary can take the place of commissions, or greatly reduce them, providing an equitable compensation scheme to both employer and employee. In today's economic

Expressing verbal appreciation of good work can mean infinitely more than monetary rewards.

and social climate, benefits have increased in perceived and real value to most employees, and with the current tax situation the owner can many times offer even more real value through benefits than in salary money itself.

And, although bonuses and other incentives can help to increase the productivity of your employees, you might want to try some less-costly methods.

Here are a few practical approaches you should consider:

1. Explain clearly what you want the employee to do. Incomplete or confusing instructions cause the employees to spend unnecessary time trying to figure out what you want them to do.

2. Be available to answer questions when they arise. This will not only keep the employees on track, but also will make you a part of their team.

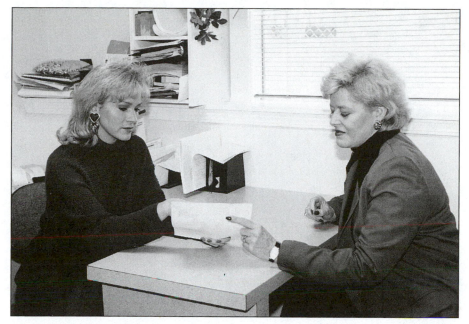

Discuss performance problems in private.

3. Be appreciative of the good work that your employees do for you. Most employees give their best effort when they know that it matters. Show them that it does. A simple "Good work," can go a long way.

4. Use tact in discussing the inadequacies of an employee's performance. Ridiculing the employee in front of others will merely cause resentment, not improved performance. If you must discuss performance problems, you should try to do so outside the presence of the employee's peers.

5. Be flexible in overseeing your employees' work. Frequently, there are many "right" ways to do a particular task. If an employee's unorthodox approach works satisfactorily, there may be no reason to ask the employee to change. If, however, you must require the employee to use a standard approach (and sometimes you must), be sure to explain *why* that approach must be used.

Taking these steps can make your business not only a more enjoyable place to work, but also a more profitable business for you.

CHAPTER THREE

Salon Structure, Image, Mission Statement, and Market Analysis

Before you can begin to think about the nuts and bolts of opening a salon, you need to have a clear image in mind of what that salon's goals and focuses should be. You might have the simplest of all goals—to earn a profit—but chances are you have a more fully developed idea of what you want the business that bears your name and reputation to be.

STRUCTURE

First, you must consider the structure of your business. Basically, there are three ways to structure your salon. Your lawyer and accountant are indispensable for their advice in this area.

It takes a lot of preplanning to decide on the image of your salon.

The easiest and most common structure (not always the best, however) is a **sole proprietorship** or **partnership**. Neither requires anything in writing legally, but a partnership agreement is recommended as a safeguard, if that is the form you elect. A proprietorship is held personally responsible for the taxes and debts of the salon. Taxes on income of $60,000 a year or higher are generally more for a sole proprietor or partners (at the time of this writing; this can change suddenly at the whim of lawmakers), and the income is reported on individual tax forms.

A **limited partnership** can be formed to limit the liability of one or more partners and to define the role and liabilities of a partner who is ordinarily only an investor and has no management responsibilities. An agreement for a limited partnership usually must be filed with the secretary of state in most states.

A **corporation** exists separate from the people who create it, becoming a legal entity unto itself. In general, corporations, especially S-Corp elections, are favorable ways of conducting business when taxable income reaches $60,000 a year or more. Personal liabilities are fewer as well.

Again, the best source of advice for how you structure your salon is your attorney and accountant. Review your situation as

PRESIDENT NYSE

PEROXIDES HAIR SALON

time passes and laws (especially tax laws) change, as the structure you operate under now may not be the most advisable down the road.

DEVELOPING A MISSION STATEMENT

Of course, everyone wants to earn money, and no business can survive without bringing in more than it spends, but there are other considerations for most of us. Developing a clear picture of what you want your business to represent makes all other planning easier. You then have a focal point to direct your planning.

The picture you envision of your salon is what you base your mission statement upon. It can be simple or complex. Most are relatively simple, sometimes as terse as one sentence.

"Our objective at *Salon du Jour* is to deliver to a discerning clientele quality hair services at a fair but premium price and to give the best possible service that we are capable of at all times."

A mission statement can literally be that concise! Indeed, brevity is desirable, keeping the intentions and philosophy to a manageable concept.

MARKET ANALYSIS

Once you have decided on a mission statement that reflects what it is you want to accomplish, your next step is to conduct a feasibility study. There exist professional companies that perform this service, but they are often costly. You can perform your own, perhaps with the help of such organizations as Service Corps of Retired Executives (SCORE) or Active Corps of Executives (ACE). All you are trying to do is determine if the salon you have in mind is possible. The feasibility study lays the groundwork for the business plan.

There are four common errors that render feasibility studies impotent, and they are:

1. A lack of realistic goals and objectives.

2. Inadequate experience (including the ability to marshal all necessary resources at the level needed).

3. Failure to anticipate problems.

4. The inability to establish a market niche. (*Business Owner's Handbook.* Indianapolis. Partners in Marketing, 1990.)

A feasibility study should:

1. Clearly define the services and products to be offered.

2. Make certain the business will be founded on accurate assumptions.

3. Be sure that the major contingencies have been provided for.

4. Ascertain that the owner has the proper expertise and/or experience to run the salon, and

5. Be certain that the profit anticipated is enough to warrant the effort and resources the business will require. (Steeblong, Rickie. *Starting Your Business.* Indianapolis. Indiana Small Business Development Center, 1991.)

Your best chances for survival and success depend on the amount of research you can do and business knowledge you can accumulate prior to actually opening a salon.

Marketing strategy is concerned with three basic questions:

• The desirability of products and services to targeted segments.

• The preferences of clientele.

• The estimation of existing competition.

These three analyses will help determine what can be sold to whom, when, how much, and at what price. A realistic estimate of these factors is crucial to your success. Lending institutions or individuals will be very interested in what you discover in this research.

CHAPTER FOUR

Site Selection

Where you locate your salon might very well be the most important business decision you can make. As the old adage goes, the three most crucial considerations an enterprise can have are... location, location, location!

Before you begin your search for the site for your salon, you should have a clear idea in mind of what your needs are, based on the market demographic you have targeted and what services and products you will be offering. All of this and the other information you need to have at your fingertips in choosing a site should be in your business plan.

Unless you obtain the best possible business location, you will face terrific odds against success. Granted, there are some salons that somehow enjoy a brisk business without much advertising, but those salons located poorly very seldom prosper. The few that do would undoubtedly do even better in a better location.

Many factors should be taken into consideration. Would the location you're considering pose an inconvenience to clients in the way of one-way streets, or will most clients be forced to make left-hand turns across the traffic flow to reach you, for instance. Will there be sufficient parking for both staff and clientele, especially during peak business hours? Is the building convenient for physically handicapped? Is the building in a safe neighborhood, and if it is, would clients have to travel through a rough area to reach you?

Other considerations include: Is the site the kind that can accommodate growth?, What will the landlord do as far as improvements are concerned?, What insurances does this particular site require that others may not?, and so on.

A good reference in helping you select your site are Small Business Administration publications *Management Aids #2.002—Locating Your Business,* or *MP10—Choosing a Retail Location.*

Before you begin visiting possible sites, you need to have a clear price range in mind, as well as size, space, and physical lay-

Location, location, location!

out requirements. In the salon business especially, you must be aware of the high cost of providing drains to shampoo and other areas that require running water. Hot water heater size is critical, as well.

For assistance in determining how much space you will need, it is helpful to consult several of your local beauty product dealers for their advice. Provide them with information they will need to give you the best estimates, such as number of employees, services and products to be offered, and timetables and plans for expansion.

You will need to understand how the cost of office space is determined. The price is usually determined first, by its location. Downtown business districts, depending on the city, may be more expensive than suburban areas, because of parking and public transportation access. Ages and conditions of buildings are also pricing factors. Listed below are various standard ways of leasing space, from the most costly to the least expensive:

- Turnkey office space in which the lessor prepares the space to fit your needs and absorbs the cost of taxes, maintenance, and janitorial services.

- Improved space in which you and the lessor negotiate modifications and maintenance costs.

- Raw space in which you (tenant) bear all the cost of modifications and maintenance.

Office space terms are usually quoted as annual rent per square foot. A space of eight hundred square feet that rents for $10 per square foot would run $8000 per year. To compute the monthly rate, merely divide $8000 by 12 (months) to arrive at $667.00.

The square footage of space is usually derived as the distance from the middle of one interior wall to the middle of the opposite interior wall, multiplied by the distance from the inside of the wall dividing the office from the hallway to the inside of the wall dividing the office from the outside.

Take a tape measure with you to measure dimensions yourself. Although most would not intentionally mislead you, space may not be measured uniformly by the owner and/or realtor.

Now you are almost ready to begin visiting sites. When you do, you should use various criteria and resources, as well as your own personal knowledge of the area. Chamber of commerce personnel can help you identify price ranges and advantages of the various high-traffic areas in the business and suburban areas. Salons in the business district have the advantage of being conve-

FAR-AHEAD STYLING SALON
SITE ASSESSMENT GUIDE

Developer ——————— Phone # ———————

Address ——————— Floor/#Location ———————

Total square feet ——————— Cost per square foot ———————

Landmarks ————————————————————

Traffic Patterns ————————————————————

Services in building or provided ————————————

Nearest salon of comparable quality ————————

External Factors	OK As Is	Needs Some Work	Needs Major Work	Questions/ Comments
Address visibility				
Ease of entrance				
Access to public transportation				
Parking space/ lighting				
Condition of parking lot				
Condition of sidewalks				
Landscaping				
Building Conditions				
Facade/Entrance				
Lobby				
Elevator/Stairs				
Hallways				

Building Conditions (cont.)	OK As Is	Needs Some Work	Needs Major Work	Questions/ Comments
Floors				
Walls/Partitions				
Windows/Glass				
Blinds/Drapes				
Lighting/Fixtures				
Rest rooms				

Office Requirements				
Sign Visibility/ Condition				
Office Layout				
Air Cond./Controls				
Heat/Controls				
Soundproofing				
Elec. Outlets				
Lighting Fixtures				
Telephone Jacks				
Storage				

Utilities/ Maintenance	Cost per Month	Install Cost	How Service Is Measured
Air Conditioning			
Electric			
Heat			
Janitorial Service			
Maintenance			
Telephone			

Utilities/ Maintenance (cont.)	Cost per Month	Install Cost	How Service Is Measured
Trash Removal			
Water			

Maintenance Service	How Often	Paid For By

Janitorial Service	How Often	Paid For By

How often is the facility painted?   Not included in Maintenance/ Janitorial Services

On the inside? _____   _____

On the outside? _____   _____

Are touch-ups done
per request? _____   _____

YES _____ NO _____   _____

nient to other businesses and may encourage walk-in business. Suburban-area salons may attract clients from both the surrounding business and residential areas.

Phone several realtors and let them know what you're looking for. Select areas that provide high traffic, but where there is little competition.

The Site Assessment Guide, adapted from a similar one Time Temporary Services uses, will help you gain the information you

Will clients find the exterior decor attractive?

need to better select a good location and negotiate your lease. As you visit locations, record your observations on this form as a guide in determining the best location.

When assessing locations, take note of these factors:

External factors. As you near the building, note:

- Visibility of the address on the building.
- Access to public transportation. (This may not be as important, depending on your targeted clientele)
- Lighting features and condition of the parking lot.
- Condition of the sidewalks.
- Landscaping and maintenance of the grounds.

Get a feel for the place. Does it look well-maintained, and is it an easy and convenient place to get in and out of? Does it look like the sort of exterior decor clients will find attractive?

Parking. This is a major consideration. Does the location provide easily accessible parking for clients? Don't forget your staff and their parking needs as well. Figure two and a half times your maximum client load at the busiest time, to allow for stylists running behind, early-arriving clients, or walk-ins for services or retail items. If an area does not provide adequate parking space, give serious consideration to looking elsewhere. Do other businesses' clients habitually use space which would be reserved for your clients should you move in, and if so, what can be done about it?

Building facade and entrance. When prospective clients or employees visit your salon, will the facade and entrance provide the quality with which you want to be associated?

Office location within the building. Obviously, it is preferable to have a salon on the first floor of a building due to its visibility and ease of access. If this is not possible, the next preference is to select a space within direct eyesight of the elevator or stairwell. One exception to this is if your city has a status address in a high-rise, but even so, building a volume business in such a site is not easy.

Lobby and hallway. The second impression a prospective client or employee has of your salon, should you elect to locate in a business building, will be obtained from the condition and decor of the lobby and hallways. Are they in optimum condition, clean, well-lighted, and attractively decorated?

Stairs and elevators. These should be in excellent condition, well-lighted, and most of all, safe.

Soundproofing. This can be important, especially if your business is close to other businesses. You can get adequate soundproofing with insulated snap-in walls, or an insulated wall placed between two outer drywall panels. Be wary of walls that are insulated only up to the ceiling. You can check how far a wall is insulated by pushing up the ceiling tile and looking into the area next to a dividing wall.

Also, because of the unpleasant odors sometimes occasioned

by our business—permanent wave solutions and nail preparations, for example—be certain that these odors will not cause a problem for other adjacent businesses.

Heating and air conditioning. The controls for each should be in your space rather than in another part of the building. If this is not the situation, but the space otherwise meets your requirements, request that the present policies regarding control of heating and air conditioning be mentioned in your lease. If there are no policies, request to have an agreement regarding heating and air conditioning control written into the lease.

Telephone capabilities. Sufficient telephone jacks will be necessary, conveniently placed for your reception area and other areas where phones are needed, as well as the capacity to add additional lines later. If you are planning on utilizing a computer, be sure the existing telephone lines can be used as computer data lines.

Electrical outlets. Make certain there are plenty of outlets for all your dryers, clippers, and other electrical apparatuses, including washers and dryers. If you plan to use equipment requiring a different voltage, such as 120 amps for tanning beds, be sure they are available. Be also certain as well that plenty of outlets will be available should you decide to remodel in the future.

Leasehold improvements. Be cognizant of whatever improvements or modifications will need to be made to create the environment you desire. Analyze the layout and space to see if there will be sufficient retail space, work space, office space, leisure space, or whatever additional needs you may have. If there is insufficient storage space, for example, you may want to add these improvements to your lease.

Janitorial and maintenance services. Check out the rest rooms! Rest rooms are one of the best signs of quality maintenance and janitorial service. Their condition will reveal to you the care the rest of the building receives. Check on the condition of the floors, carpets, walls and windows. Find out who is responsible for maintenance and janitorial services and if any of these services are provided.

TO NEGOTIATE A LEASE

Now, you're almost done. You've found the best possible location at what seems to be the best deal. This is a crucial time. Don't just sit down and sign whatever lease the landlord hands you. It is advisable to consult an attorney to review the lease also. The Lease Checklist, provided below, can assist you during the negotiating period. Things you will want to discuss and get in writing are:

Option to sublet. Insist up front that your lease give you the right to sublet the space if you should need more room in the future. If no more space is available in the same building, you should have the right to move where you can grow.

Noncompete clause. Require your lease to include a section preventing another similar salon from renting in your building or area owned by the same company (such as a mall), unless you deem the mall large enough to support other salons of the same quality as yours. If the lessor balks at such a section, ask to put in a clause that would nullify your obligation to the lease should another salon of similar quality lease space in your proximity.

Heating and air conditioning. If the controls are not located in your space and under your control, make an agreement describing the temperature control and add it to the lease. Also, clarify how the electricity will be measured and who pays for it.

Signs. Make sure of the type of sign, lettering, and copy allowed. Finding out after you've signed the lease that the sign you had in mind isn't allowed can not only be frustrating, but costly.

Maintenance and janitorial services. Compare the costs between owner-provided services and your own independently contracted services. Have any arrangements specified in definite terms.

Concessions. See if you can negotiate with the owner to pay for any costs incurred should improvements or modifications need to be made to the property before your opening day, covering such things as installing electrical outlets or light fixtures, painting, erecting tables or counters, or carpeting. Get permission to remove items such as air conditioners or water coolers should you plan to change their locations.

Contingency clause. Request a contingency clause that states you will not be responsible for the lease terms if you don't receive your salon license within a specific amount of time. Snafus have occurred, believe it or not, and you don't want to be paying rent on space you can't legally use.

Ninety-day cancellation notice. Standard notification of renewal or cancellation of leases usually is sixty days. Negotiate to increase this period to ninety days to give additional time to make a wise decision about your location.

Again, be sure to have your attorney review the lease prior to signing it, and always obtain everything in writing. Verbal assurances, promises and guarantees normally do not hold up legally should a dispute arise.

FAR-AHEAD STYLING SALON
LEASE CHECKLIST

Costs $_____

Monthly rent	_____	Heating & A/C Agreement
# Square feet	_____	_____
Cost per sq. ft.	_____	_____
Security deposit	_____	_____
Monthly taxes	_____	_____
Other deposits	_____	Sign Placement &
Other expenses	_____	Maintenance Agreement
Total	$_____	_____
		_____
		_____
Terms		_____
Date lease to begin	_____	Maintenance & Janitorial
Length of lease	_____	Agreement
Option to renew at		_____
same rate	_____	_____

Terms (continued)	Maintenance & Janitorial Agreement (continued)
Option to sublet _____	_____
First choice on	_____
additional space _____	_____
Noncompete clause _____	Concessions
90-day cancellation	Prior to the beginning lease
notice _____	date, the owner will make the
Contingency clause _____	following modifications:
All lease terms are in writing	_____
and have been reviewed by my	_____
lawyer.	_____
Signed _____	_____

The location of your salon is going to be one of the most, if not the single most, important factor in its success. Spend the time to do proper research in this area. Don't grab the first location that looks reasonably good, but be thorough in selecting the place where you'll conduct business for at least the next several years, depending on the length of your lease.

CHAPTER FIVE

When to Hire—When to Fire

Knowing when to expand by increasing your staff and, conversely, knowing when it is in the best interests of the business to decrease staff are two of the most important elements of maintaining a successful bottom line.

Financially, adding staff members may fall into the category of "taking two steps back to take one giant step forward." What this means is that by hiring additional staff, at first you may experience only an increase in overhead while your gross sales remain the same. The expectation, however, is that such a move will eventually increase not only the gross but the net profit the salon will realize. On the other hand, there are times when letting a stylist or other staff member go may result in an initial loss of income but will be better for the long-range plans and well-being of the business.

Add an employee if the following conditions exist in your salon:

- The market demands a skill the salon doesn't possess.

- There are tasks you are currently performing that can be delegated to an individual in order to free your time for more profitable tasks.

- You are not finding enough time to effectively run your salon.

- You are unable to service your customers to their satisfaction.

- You can devote sufficient time and thought to the selection of a new employee.

- There are skilled and experienced individuals available, or trainable individuals with little or no experience.

Clock-watching and punctuality are not the same thing.

General characteristics that should be apparent in a candidate would be flexibility and willingness to work hard, ability to comprehend and carry out instructions, thoroughness, maturity and a desire to learn.

There are also times when business volume indicates it would be a good move to add personnel, but you don't think you would enjoy the added responsibility and managerial duties necessary to supervise others. If this is the case, then one of the best ways to increase income is by raising fees, provided you have sufficient business to warrant that strategy. The marketplace will determine if you are able to do so. Other means of remaining the same size and increasing profits are to "work smarter" by various methods, which may include taking less time to perform services, hiring only assistants instead of full-time (and full-salaried) staff, working longer hours or more days, increasing marketing efforts, decreasing overhead, and using similar tactics.

For the purposes of this book, we are going to assume you desire to grow bigger and increase both gross sales and net profits by adding staff.

Now, when and how do you determine staff expansion? Rather than doing so based merely on a "gut feeling," or because you're just too busy and need help, you can use formulas and guidelines provided here to make sound decisions.

First, if you increase your annual totals by $100,000 but your overhead costs you as much or more than your increase, you've lost money. If you see, however, that such a move will eventually lead to a higher profit, then it may be a good move. This is an instance when taking two steps back to take one giant step forward may be advisable. Although this is sometimes the only way to increase staff size, it is obviously better to realize a higher profit margin immediately. If this is not possible and you are still determined to add staff, be certain you can project and have enough cash flow to sustain your operation during this period. Otherwise, you may have to reduce staff under less than favorable conditions, for you as well as the employees let go. Psychologically and financially, this most likely will produce a detrimental effect.

For a new employee to be profitable, he or she must bring in enough to provide a profit of 15 to 20% over the cost of performing the service. When figuring employee cost, don't make the mistake of thinking "Well, I pay on a commission of 50%, so that means on a $20.00 service I just made 50% or $10.00." This is a means of arithmetic that will add up to only one thing—business failure!

The cost of each employee amounts to much more than the commission paid to that employee. You have many other factors to weigh in, starting with the commission paid. For instance, you will have to provide additional space for that employee to perform his or her services. Costs for such items as utilities will be higher. Time spent in supervising has a monetary value. Additional taxes such as the company's contribution to that employee's Social Security and other benefits have to be figured in, as well as the effect on the salon's and your own personal taxes which will be impacted by a higher gross income. Additional advertising and marketing efforts for that person are an element. And what about the inevitable disgruntled client you get with new employees (no matter how talented and able), who will need a refund or extra time (worth money) to satisfy?

Clearly, there is much more to the cost of a new employee than simply the commission or salary paid! To ignore these factors is foolhardy.

Just as there are business reasons to hire additional staff, there are also compelling reasons to terminate personnel. There are basically three valid reasons for letting someone go:

1. The employee *won't* do the job.

2. The employee *can't* do the job.

3. The employee is *negative* and spreads the disease throughout the salon.

Does the employee maintain proper courtesy to clients? Negative traits are diseases easily transmitted throughout the salon.

If you have such an individual that cannot or will not improve attitude, work ethic and/or job performance, especially in a small salon, you have no logical choice but to terminate the employee. One ineffective staff member may cost a salon 25 percent of its productivity.

It is a good idea, if possible, to have the terminated employee sign a voluntary resignation letter, which may protect you from unemployment benefits claims. Here is an example of such a letter:

I, _____, hereby submit my voluntary resignation, effective as of _____.

   I am resigning because

   _____ I have obtained another position.

   _____ I am relocating.

   _____ I am entering a new field.

   _____ I feel I am unsuited for my present position.

   _____ I wish to increase my income.

   _____ Other. _____

_____   _____
Date   Employee Signature

Immediately ask the employee to remove personal items and tools from the workplace. Arrange for the employee to receive a final paycheck. Cancel all benefits and advise about any conversion privileges, such as with insurances. Conduct an exit interview to learn how to keep good employees. (If the person is averse to this, ask for a letter detailing what you could have done to avoid the situation.) Try to have the employee leave on as good terms as possible.

In many salons, when a staff member leaves or is discharged, the company policy is to inform all those phoning in for that person's

When an employee leaves, ask him or her to sign a voluntary letter of resignation.

services that the stylist is no longer with the company and they don't know where he or she is presently employed. This is totally unprofessional and not worthy of a quality salon. Instead, tell the caller you are sorry the particular stylist is no longer with the salon, but you are certain the caller would be happy if you could book her with another stylist. If the person still asks for the discharged stylist's new workplace, pass it on if you know it. (In our own salon, we attempt to go a step beyond this, volunteering the information before the client even asks, and cheerfully giving the caller the phone number, although we make sure to invite the client back into the salon with another designer.)

Don't allow discharged employees to retain keys to the salon, or access to any records, client files, or information of that sort. Those items are salon property and not available to discharged staff. It is good to inform new stylists of this policy when you first bring them on board.

The best defense against having to fire employees is to take every step possible to hire the proper ones to begin with!

Again, as termination goes, there is no formula, but when confronted with a personnel problem in the salon, the role of the owner-manager can be summarized in the following steps:

- Identify and document the problem.

- Initiate the confrontation with the employee.

- If the employee is fired, make sure the personnel file contains documentation substantiating the employee's shortcomings and failure to take corrective action. Your company should have a periodic evaluation procedure documenting each individual's job performance. Employees should be required to sign or initial evaluations as evidence that they are aware of the contents.

- If a terminated employee has signature authority over company bank accounts, withdraw such authority immediately and notify bank authorities.

- Make sure all company property in the employee's possession is returned (office keys, credit cards, tools, computers, files, etc.). Consider the necessity of changing appropriate access codes and passwords to the company computer system.

- Review fringe benefit programs to ensure compliance with notification requirements allowing continuing coverage upon termination of employment.

- When notifying other employees, customers, and others of the employee's termination, avoid libelous or slanderous remarks.

- Finally, don't let terminated employees linger. For your protection and theirs, accompany them from termination to their departure.

Finally, your hiring and firing practices and your personnel manual should be reviewed by an attorney who is knowledgeable about labor law.

CHAPTER SIX

How to Price Products Profitably

Retailing your product lines properly is crucial to a salon's bottom line. *Properly*, in this case, refers to pricing products in such a manner as to assure a reasonable profit. Improper pricing of the products you offer for resale to your clientele can be disastrous to the financial health of the business. It can ultimately lead to the hairstyling concern being forced to close its doors, or, at best, struggle along with a marginally profitable enterprise.

The great majority of salons simply charge what the manufacturer, distributor, or dealer recommends. While this *can* be the proper price for some, if not many, salons, it can also be a totally unrealistic figure for *your* operation, with your own unique set of

Nice...but not the shrewdest businessperson.

Retail prices need to provide a fair profit.

factors contributing to the *real* cost of the product or products you offer for sale on your shelves. It should be noted, however, that most manufacturers and distributors keep a sharp eye on what they suggest as a retail price for their products. They are acutely aware of salon expenses and what it takes in most cases for the salon owner to turn a profit. However, your particular situation may be different. That is why it is important to perform your own study to insure that the price you charge for products is sufficient to provide a fair profit for your own situation.

Keep in mind that from a sales point of view what is important in assessing the price of a particular product, which will enable you to move products from your display into the hands of consumers, is *not* the value of the product (whatever that is!). What is important is the perceived value of that bottle of shampoo or conditioner. **Perceived value** is the determining factor in the consumer's decision-making process. You can stick virtually any price you wish on a particular product and sell that product, so long as the purchaser conceives that to be a fair price for the value received.

To reiterate: Value of the product is essentially meaningless. Drill this point home. What *is* important is the perceived value the product has in the marketplace. If you can find a similar-quality product at a lower cost that has a similar perceived value with your clientele, you can maintain your markup percentage and create a bona fide bargain for your clients, causing profits to rise through volume. Or, you can increase your markup percentage, in which instance your volume will probably not increase significantly, but your profits will as you have increased your gross margin. The other side of the coin is that if the perceived value is lower in customers' eyes, sales may drop even if prices are lower. Just remember: People buy perceived value, not actual value, whether you are talking retail or service sales.

How, do you suppose, can two restaurants in the same town offer virtually the identical meal with the ingredients costing each restaurant the same, but for significantly different prices...and both restaurants enjoy a healthy business? Simple—patrons of each *perceive* the value of the meal to be what the restaurant presents it to be. A hamburger may cost $1.50 in one establishment and $3.50 in the other one, and both are busy! Of course, there are differences in the quality of meat, buns and condiments available to each, but assuming they both buy the same ingredients from the same suppliers, what makes the difference in the customer's eyes? One thing and one thing only—their perception of the value (to them) of that meal.

There are other factors at work hat help determine that perception. The ambiance, for instance. The cheaper hamburger may be sold in a "joint" with little or no "atmosphere," surly or nonexistent waiters or waitresses, and a fry cook, in full view, flipping the burgers, clad in a torn T-shirt, while the more-pricy hamburger is served at a fancy table setting, by a polite serviceperson, while pleasing music gently serenades your ears. In each restaurant, the meal is essentially the same—oh, you may get a sprig of parsley at one and not the other—but, depending on your particular desires at the moment, you will pay either price without qualms or argument. The difference in each instance is the perceived value...

Now, of course, our products are different. The consumer may be very aware that the bottle of shampoo you are offering at $8.00 can be gotten at another salon for less and may, indeed, elect to make her purchases there, so we have to take that into consideration, but if the shampoo is being sold at a price that negates any profit, do you really want to follow in that salon's footsteps? Only if you are operating a nonprofit foundation! And, even nonprofit foundations must maintain a balance in the black or they will go under, as any other business would.

Sometimes, after careful research, it is determined that you can more profitably sell your products even *cheaper* than the suggested retail price. By using the formulas and pricing strategies presented in this chapter, you will be able to determine just what your selling price should be, and each product can then carry a price tag that will lead to a profit on that item.

There are three basic factors that influence the profitability of retail sales: **gross volume sales, gross profit margins**, and **overhead expenses**. We will go into each factor and show you how to figure each so that you arrive at a plus in your ledger. Two of these components can be controlled—overhead expenses and gross profit margins. Not as much control can be maintained over gross sales as they can be influenced only by your marketing efforts, so your planning should give the most consideration to overhead and gross profit margins. Once you have done your research in these areas, you may well find that the suggested retail price is way out of line with your goals, and, if you do what most salons do and blindly use that price, you may find yourself in the same situation as those other salons and lose money on your sales. If you determine the profit is not sufficient at the suggested retail price, it is probably time to consider finding different sources for those products at a lower cost, or seeking more profitable lines, or even implementing your own, personalized line or lines. Remember: it is no more your function as a salon to provide an outlet and profit for distributors than it is to provide jobs for others. Your *only* business goal as a salon should be to realize a profit for the salon. If those other things happen as a result of the way you do business (and they will, if you use solid business tactics), and if you do enable the product distributor to achieve a profit and provide a job for others, then that's nice, but those are not the reasons a business exists. A business's sole *raison d'etre* is to provide a reasonable profit for the owners of that business for the time expended.

You should be aware of some common mistakes made by salon owners in purchasing, stocking and pricing their inventory as you begin to determine pricing.

Significant amounts of inventory left languishing on the shelves or in the back room can eat up any profit margin quickly. The cost factor in storage and length of time before a product sells carries a monetary value. You pay for the space those products occupy in a variety of ways, including the rent or mortgage payment, the cost of someone's wages to unpack the products, stick a price tag on it, put it on the shelf or in the storeroom, dust it periodically, rotate it, move it, and even to erect the display unit! If you borrowed money to purchase inventory, you have another factor to consider in the price (interest) you paid for the use of the money borrowed. You will pay yourself or an employee to ring up the sale once it has been purchased, and most salons pay a sales commission to the

Stock languishing in the back room eats up profits.

stylist who made the sale. You pay utilities such as electricity, gas, heat and air conditioning. Both property and sales taxes are assessed, and perhaps other taxes peculiar to your state and parish or county. You may advertise or promote your products. Inflation eats away while the clock is ticking on that unsold bottle of shampoo. You could have invested the same amount of money in another investment that would be making you money. There are dozens of factors that influence the true cost of that bottle of shampoo, and if all you are taking into account are its cost from the distributor, the sales commission paid and one or two other considerations, you may have erred greatly in its proper pricing. You may have already begun the process of losing money on the item the very day you stuck it on the shelf, even though it sold five minutes later!

Those "deals" that manufacturers and dealers offer at trade shows may seem amazingly attractive and sensible, and maybe they are, but always keep in mind that the sale price is only one

Remember: the sale price is only one part of the equation.

part of the equation. All the other factors we have named are important as well, and need to be computed to arrive at a sound buying decision at these buying opportunities. Based on your past experience, you should have an idea how long it will take to move that "deal" out of the salon in the retail bags of your clients. When you analyze all the factors, perhaps that wonderful "One-Time-Only, One-Third-Off, Acme-Show Discount" isn't so wonderful after all. Only by taking all the factors involved into account will you know for sure what kind of bargain it is.

Sometimes, it is great. And sometimes it isn't. Often, it is shrewder to pay a higher price and maintain a smaller inventory than it is to purchase that huge amount at a reduced initial cost. Another wise option might be to see if it is possible to form a loose consortium of salons in your area to purchase the "deal" under one salon's name. Each salon would then take a share of the deal proportionate to their needs, thereby achieving the fantastic low price per unit, but eliminating the disadvantage of too-large amounts of inventory sitting idle and eroding profit margins.

Many times, discounts are offered for timely payments. To see if that would be a good deal for your salon, follow this example which provides the proper calculation to determine what you actually save:

Example: You have placed an order for $1,000 that is due in 30 days. The vendor has given you terms of 2/10/net 30. This means that if you pay the invoice within 10 days, you will get a 2% discount or the order will only cost you $980 ($1,000 × 2% = $20). You have the option of either missing the 2% discount on an order that cost you $1,000 or borrowing the money at 8%. Here is the calculation:

P = Principal

IR = Interest Rate

D = Number of Days

P × IR × D = Interest Charge

$980 × 8% × 20/365 = Interest Charge

(The principal is $980 because you will be taking advantage of the discount.)

(Interest will be charged for 20 days because it is assumed that the invoice would be paid net 30.)

$4.30 = Interest Charge

Therefore, your savings is $15.70. (The discount of $20 less the $4.30 interest cost.)

INVENTORY CONTROL

The first step in establishing control of your inventory is to set up an inventory control system. Your accountant can be of tremendous help here, provided he or she is familiar with your type of operation (If he or she is not, consider the services of one who is!) Computers are invaluable in this phase of salon operation, and are indeed becoming not a luxury but almost a necessity. Many excellent computer inventory systems are out there at a reasonable cost. Bar coding computer program capabilities for larger salons (and even smaller ones that move a lot of products) should be considered. (See Chapter Twelve, "Computers" for in-depth information.)

The main function of an inventory system is a means by which you can identify and track retail and us items. Numbering systems, usually a one- to five-character mnemonic, that represents each item in your inventory, are standard. Even if you opt for a noncomputer system, such a numbering system will make the transition much easier to a software system later on, as most are based on such numbering systems. Computerized cash drawers can be used, as well. The following is an example of such a system, using conditioners as an example:

ITEM NAME AND SIZE	INVENTORY CODE
8 oz. Bold Strokes Moist. Cond.	100
16 oz. Bold Strokes Moist. Cond.	101
8 oz. Bold Strokes Reconditioner	102
16 oz. Bold Strokes Reconditioner	103
8 oz. Bold Strokes Cond. Dry Hair	104
16 oz. Bold Strokes Cond. Dry Hair	105

You then need to establish minimum and maximum stock levels, the minimum representing the number of stock at which you will reorder. This can be done in longhand if you are using a manual system, though a software program will adjust it automatically, saving time. A physical inventory of all retail and usage stock needs to be taken at regular intervals, perhaps weekly. Then purchases can be made for those items reaching minimum levels. Another advantage of this is that losses due to pilferage and theft can be discovered and steps can then be taken to correct the problem.

Also included in your system should be information on distributors, the wholesale unit price, and the retail price you have established.

Count sheets for physically counting inventory should include information such as the inventory code and description, vendors, minimum-maximum inventory levels, the on-hand count and the inventory class (group of items of the same type, such as conditioners).

This system will give you information such as total salon sales of a particular product, total sales in a single class, total product sales, vendor purchases in a single class and total vendor purchases. Systems should be set up so that individual totals can be obtained easily, as well. Usage figures will tell you salon total use of a product, of a class of products, overall usage total, and individual totals. When a stylist uses a product at the backbar or shampoo area, he or she should check out that item so that you can track it, thereby determining waste and overusage of products by stylists. This also serves as a psychological barrier to waste products, as the stylist is aware that his or her use of products is being monitored.

By comparing usage and sales figures for various periods you will get a clear picture of who is improving in sales and who is not. With this knowledge, you can set realistic goals, knowing the history and patterns of both figures, for the salon and for individual stylists.

When you determine items that are not moving well, you are then able to take necessary action. You may decide that items remaining on the shelves too long should be returned to the dealer for a refund or credit, letting you then use that resource for other products that move faster. Or, you could make that product a sale item to spur sales. Other options may include moving the particular product to a different location as this sometimes makes a difference, or deciding to offer your staff additional motives to sell the item, in the form of a higher commission for that item or a bonus or prize of some sort. The point is, you should be able to determine, by proper tracking, that some action is called for, rather than allowing the product to continue to lose money for you by sitting on the shelf.

Stylists' sales should be tracked individually. This will tell you where sales are weak, by stylist, and steps can be taken to improve the situation.

Get a handle on what you have in the salon, who and what is selling, and what is just sitting there, acting as a cancer on profits.

Be sure you know the difference between markup and profit, which are two different figures entirely. If you buy an item for $1.00 and sell it for $1.43, you have a 43% **markup**, but your **profit margin** (this is gross, not net) on the item is only 30%, because although $.43 is 43% of $1.00, it is only 30% of $1.43. This is *very* important to understand! Knowing this will enable you to calculate how many of a particular product you will need to sell to make the equation balance. Also, lower overhead, higher sales volume, or a higher or lower markup percentage will each alter the equation and result in a plus or minus profit for the salon.

Now, here is what you should be looking at in order to price your products. This list is meant to be inclusive, but there may be other factors at work in your own situation, so use the formulas provided, but also learn to search out and identify other cost factors. Conversely, not all the factors named here may apply to your salon, so disregard those that do not.

Listed below are the basic factors at work in most cases, which need to be figured into the pricing formula:

- Dealer cost per item

- Sales commissions paid

- Rent or mortgage payment on space utilized for products (item took what % of paid-for space?)

- Advertising and promotions

- Retail bags

- Maintenance of product, including wages to pay for services of unpacking, pricing, storing, dusting, placement, inventorying, accounting and record keeping, and ringing sales up

- Time between purchase and resale (what would the same amount of money have earned if used for a conservative investment instead?)

- Taxes—inventory taxes, property taxes, sales taxes and more

- Raises in purchase price that occurred after your purchase and before you sold the item

- Inflation costs

- Theft and pilferage

- Usage waste

- Shipping, postage and handling

- Size or quantity offered

- Interest payable on financial purchases

- Miscellaneous

As quickly becomes evident, there is more to pricing than just computing the purchase price and perhaps the stylist's commission and arriving at a markup price. It becomes even more evident that the manufacturer's suggested retail price may be grossly inadequate for your situation. These are arrived at by the manufacturer for the nation in general and cannot possibly take into account local factors such as rents and utilities, nor, for that matter, other cost factors you face. Note the operative word in the phrase "*suggested* retail price"! It is possible they are suggesting such retail prices based on an ideal situation, on what a perfectly run salon should charge to create a profit. There are few of those!

Or, perhaps it is even possible such "suggested" prices are set in somewhat the same way as the point spreads on pro football games are set in Las Vegas—arbitrarily—to attract an equal number of bettors for both sides and having no relation to reality or expected outcomes! In any case, it behooves the prudent salon owner to get a handle on what is real for his or her salon, and not on what some freshly minted MBA in California has dreamed up.

Set product prices to produce a reasonable profit.

This sounds like manufacturer-bashing, but it is really not. The manufacturers of our products have made available many fine products that have greatly enhanced our profession, and we think they would be the first to advise stylists to set prices that provide a reasonable profit to their salons. If it were not for the many fine advances manufacturers are responsible for, our profession would be light years away from where we are today. Most of our education and many of or techniques were given us either by product manufacturers or under their sponsorship. Just keep in mind that when they suggest prices, it is only meant to be a rough guide for the stylist. If those figures lead to unprofitability in many salons, they will be hurt as well. Indeed, many of us who have been providing cosmetology services for a long time can remember companies that ended up entering the supermarket retail arena. It may be possible they did so because the salon market became unprofitable for them, and...perhaps that was due in part to unrealistic "suggested retail prices" stylists blindly followed.

The fact remains that if you are not pricing your retail items prudently, you are not going to be buying from the dealer for very long and that is a situation that does no one—manufacturer, dealer, or stylist—any good.

There are three basic factors that influence the profitability of retail sales: gross volume sales, gross profit margins, and overhead expenses. Overhead expenses can be further broken down into two categories: expenses that are **fixed** and those that are **variable**. Fixed expenses are those costs that "march on" whether the door swings open that day or not. They include rent, debt service (including interest), and insurance. Variable costs are those costs incurred as a sale is consumated. These costs include labor, supplies, and the majority of utilities. The important point is that they are *all* controllable.

Now that you have a grasp of the determinants that are involved, we shall see how to use those factors in arriving at profitable retail prices. We will use a specific example, a bottle of shampoo, to illustrate several formulas that can be used for proper pricing. Using these as a models, you can then extrapolate them to all products.

MARKETING FORMULAS

Inventory Item: 8 oz. bottle of Bubble Tickle Shampoo

Suggested Retail Price: $ 8.00

Cost From Dealer: $ 4.00

Example #1—Calculating the selling price using the markup based on *cost*.

The buyer of Bubble Tickle Shampoo desires to set the selling price. It has been standard policy to mark up new merchandise at 66 2/3% of cost. Determine the selling price at a cost of $4.00 as follows:

Formula: $S = C (1 + R)$ where   S = Selling price
C = Cost
R = Markup % based on cost

Solution: $S = C (1 + R)$
$S = 4 (1 + .66\ 2/3)$
$S = 4 (1.666)$
$S = \$\ 6.66$

Example #2—Calculating the selling price based on the *gross profit margin* it produces.

You have paid $4.00 for a bottle of Bubble Tickle Shampoo. If the gross margin you wish to realize is 55% based on the selling price, determine the selling price of the product by using the following formula:

Formula: S = C / (1 – R) where   S = Selling price
                                    C = Cost
                                    R = Markup % based on
                                        selling price

Solution: S = C / (1 – R)
           S = 4 / (1 – .55)
           S = 4 / .45
           S = $8.88

Example #3—Calculating the selling price based on a *loaded selling price*. For instance, a load factor would be defined as a percentage of the sales price that would be used to pay the expense of a sales commission.

You desire to establish a selling price for a bottle of Bubble Tickle Shampoo so as to yield a 55% gross profit rate, computed after paying a 15% sales commission to a stylist. The cost to purchase the bottle is $4.00. To determine the selling price:

Formula: S = C / 1 – (R + r) where   S = Selling price
                                       C = Cost
                                       R = Markup % based on
                                           selling price
                                       r = Load factor

Solution: S = C / 1 – (R + r)
           S = 4 / 1 – (.55 + .15)
           S = 4 / 1 – .70
           S = 4 / .3
           S = $13.33

Example #4—Calculating the selling price based on a markup based on *cost*. This formula will allow you to calculate the selling price allowing for the payment of a load factor (see example #3) and retain the same gross profit on sales.

You desire to maintain your usual markup based on a determined selling price. You pay a 10% commission to a stylist for the sale of

Example #4 (cont.)

Bubble Tickle. The cost to purchase the bottle is $4.00 and the usual markup based on cost is 45%. To determine the selling price:

Formula: $S = C (1 + R) / (1 - r)$ S = Selling price
where: C = Cost
                                             R = Markup % based on cost
                                             r = Load factor

Solution: $S = C (1 + R) / (1 - r)$
            $S = 4 (1 + .45) / (1 - .1)$
            $S = 4 (1.45) / .9$
            $S = 5.80 / .9$
            $S = \$6.44$

BREAKEVEN POINT

Determining the product breakeven point is essential. To understand breakeven sales you need to become familiar with several terms.

Fixed Costs

Fixed expenses are those costs that are incurred whether the products had been sold or not. For example, rent will continue to be payable whether or not any products have been sold. The expense is not contingent upon the sale of products.

Variable Costs

Variable costs are contingent upon the sale of the product. As the product is sold, variable costs are incurred. For example, the sales commission payable to a stylist is only payable in connection with a sale. If there is no sale, there is no sales commission to pay.

Net Sales

Net sales are computed by subtracting from gross sales any sales discounts, returns and allowances, and sales tax collected.

Breakeven Sales

Breakeven sales occur at the point at which net sales equals costs. All sales after this are **profit sales**.

The formula used to determine your product's breakeven sales is as follows:

Formula: BE = FE / (1 – V/S) where:	BE = Breakeven FE = Fixed costs V = Variable costs S = Net sales

Example: The following data was taken from your company's accounting ledger as it relates to Bubble Tickle Shampoo.

Net Sales   **$3,000**

	Total	Fixed	Variable
Purchases of product	$1,000		$1,000
Labor—Product-related	500		500
Selling Expenses	200		200
Allocated Expenses	600	500	100
Totals	**$2,300**	**$500**	**$1,800**

Solution: BE = FE / (1 – (V/S))
BE = 500 / (1 – (1,800/3,000))
BE = 500 / (1 – .6)
BE = 500 / .4
BE = $1,250

Inventory Turnover

Data is abstracted for activity in Bubble Tickle Shampoo

Beginning Inventory	$ 1,500
Purchases During the Year	1,000
Cost of Goods Available for Sale	$ 2,500
Less Ending Inventory	500
Cost of Goods Sold	**$ 2,000**

Inventory Turnover (cont.)

Formula: $T = C / ((IB + IE) / 2)$ T = Inventory turnover
                                         C = Cost of goods sold
                                         IB = Beginning inventory
                                         IE = Ending inventory

Solution: $T = C / ((IB + IE) / 2)$
          $T = 2000 / ((1500 + 500) / 2)$
          $T = 2000 / (2000 / 2)$
          $T = 2000 / 1000$
          $T = 2$ Times

A good accounting system is essential to the success of your business. It is the foundation of decisions that will be made about the direction your business should take, the achievement of goals, and the establishment of priorities. A good accounting system makes you "accountable" for your actions or lack thereof.

A good accounting system is the best defense in the event of an Internal Revenue Service audit. The burden of proof for deductions and the reporting of income is the responsibility of the taxpayer.

A good accounting system enables the user to categorize cash inflows and outflows for the determination of net income or loss; it is the basis for setting goals in the determination of future expenses (i.e. budget), and it provides a history of the business' activity to calculate formulas.

Your most important partner is your accountant!

CHAPTER SEVEN

How to Price Services Profitably

Services are the backbone of any salon's business, providing the major source of income for most salons. It is advisable to create as much demand as possible for products, but we are a *service* business primarily, and it is services offered and performed that provide the greater part of cash flow and profits.

Pricing services properly so as to insure a profit is therefore critical, and should be studied carefully and reevaluated periodically as the economic climate changes, making certain that the pricing structure always is conducive to providing a bottom line in the black.

A common mistake in pricing services is to imitate competitors, or to simply adopt the pricing strategy of a salon you previously worked in. This can be disastrous if the pricing structure imitated has not been well thought out, which may well be the case. Chances are the pricing strategy emulated was chosen originally in much the same way—itself copied or taken from a similar source—and all you will be doing is duplicating a system not favorable to a profit.

Indiana University's Bobby Knight, one of the most successful basketball coaches in history, bases his coaching philosophy upon a simple premise that his teams don't play "other teams"; they "play against themselves." In other words, they attempt to play against a high standard of excellence they have established for themselves, and by doing so, the victories will take care of themselves. Such a strategy would work well in any salon's pricing strategy. Set up a standard of performance each stylist within the salon always attempts to reach, and price that performance fairly.

Ours is a highly subjective profession, with vast ranges of abilities, talents, and work ethics, and as such is more open to a greater range of prices for the services we perform than most other fields. Letting other stylists' or salons' prices be the determinant

Price services to insure profit.

in our pricing structure can easily lower our own expectations, goals, and ultimately, profits. If, however, you continually work to the best of your ability and always strive to raise your standards and increase those abilities, *and* charge a correspondingly fair price, you will not only increase greatly the odds of recording a profit each year, but will also increase your own self-esteem and pride in your craft. Such feelings translate into even better work…and more income. A positive cycle indeed!

How long do you think your work will remain top quality when you feel your haircut is worth $50.00 and you only charge $30.00, because that is what your last salon charged? Maybe a month. Probably not that long. And then, your attitude will decline and close behind it your work will begin to reflect that attitude. Before you know it, you will no longer be putting out a $50.00 haircut but one that more accurately reflects the price charged or, more than likely, an even worse product. It becomes a self-fulfilling prophecy. Those who are paid less than what they perceive themselves and their work to be worth end up lowering the quality of that work to the point that it matches the payment received. Mary, my wife and business partner, has an accurate saying in describing such underachievers, remarking that such individuals "keep bumping their heads on their own ceilings."

If you must create ceilings to bump your head on, make the ceiling extraordinarily high!

Competitors' prices *are* an important factor in arriving at your own prices, but be sure the salon or person whose prices you are thinking of emulating is indeed a competitor, and not just someone who has a salon in the same geographical proximity. Compare apples to apples, not apples to oranges. A Burger Chef may be located a block from the famous Four Seasons, but they are not competitors except in the very narrow sense that they both serve edible foodstuffs. This is not a pejorative comparison of either restaurant—both establishments are hugely successful at creating the markets they serve; but that is the key—they each attract a much different clientele—and that is what you must do to become successful. Determine your market and price your services accordingly. If you think your talents and philosophy work better in a "fast food" type of market arena, then by all means price your services and plan your strategy accordingly. If, on the other hand, you perceive your services to be on a higher plane, then don't apply fast food prices and principles to your enterprise.

Even when you consider true competitor's prices when setting your own, don't let this be the only factor weighed in the equation. How do you know their prices will lead to profitability in your situation? The answer, of course, is that you don't, until you study all the pertinent factors involved. It is safe to say that even if most of the contributing factors are equal, it would be unlikely that every single price your competitor charges would be profitable in your situation.

You must figure what your own costs will be and what you feel would be a reasonable profit, and only then can you come up with the pricing structure necessary to achieve your goals.

FORMULA TO BASE SERVICE PRICES ON

Here is a basic formula to base prices on.

A salon's compensation policy should be designed to accomplish three primary objectives. It needs to attract qualified staff, retain employees, and recognize and reward the performance of high-quality work. A service business can be divided into three segments. They are:

1. Cost of labor

2. Overhead

3. Owner profit

The rule of thumb to determine the amount you should charge for an employee's time is 3 to 3.5 times the employee's labor cost. Direct labor cost includes paid benefits and working-condition fringes. Therefore, if an employee's labor cost for the service is $5.00, the service should be charged at $15.00 to $17.50 (service value).

FORMULA

Service Value $= SV$

Labor cost $= L$

Multiple (employee's time) $= 3.5$

Solution: $SV = L \times M$
$SV = \$5.00 \times 3.5$
$SV = \$17.50$

The formula could be used in the inverse to determine labor cost where:

$SV = L \times M$
$L = SV / M$

Solution: $L = SV / M$
$L = \$17.50 / 3.5$
$L = \$5.00$

A PSYCHOLOGICAL DYNAMIC

Remember, too, that there is a psychological dynamic at work in salon prices. Don't make the mistake of discounting this dynamic. As in any other business, the successful entrepreneur will charge what the market will bear. The marketplace is the great leveler and determiner of a correct pricing structure. If the marketplace doesn't think your services are worth the prices charged, you'll find out soon enough! It is your job as the salon owner to convince enough members of the buying public that the prices affixed to your services are worth it. Always remember—**perceived value** is what is always paramount in pricing…and it is up to *you* to create that perception.

There is a psychological effect at work in any business with an artistic element to it. You can even call it the "snob effect," and it is a two-edged sword. Some clients love to drop the name (and the prices) of the high-priced salon they frequent. Another type of client is enamored of a kind of "reverse snobbery," taking pride in the fact that they *don't* pay what they consider high prices, imply-

Perceived value is always the most important factor in pricing, but it must be a shared perception among a sufficient number of the market to render a profit.

ing that they are superior buyers, smart enough not to pay exorbitant fees. The snob effect or its reverse can work well for different markets.

Reverse snob appeal has been used with great effectiveness by national television and magazine ad campaigns for home permanent kits in which the message was that consumers who purchased the kit were of higher intelligence because they paid much less for a product that was the equal of a high-priced salon service. There is no doubt this campaign worked for the market segment the company was after.

On the other hand, a leading salon chain ran highly effective ads with the opposite message, showing a woman with a hair disaster obtained from using such kits and then showing the gorgeous, sophisticated style one of its clients received in the salon. Both approaches were successful, and actually for the same reasons. They both appealed to a snob effect—one reverse, the other direct.

Understand and use the psychology of prices. It exists.

RAISING PRICES

Another area of pricing that is almost always sensitive with stylists is the question of when and how much to raise prices. We have a tendency to become friends with our clients, and that is all well and good, except if it interferes with properly pricing services and raising those prices when they should be raised. Many times we have the uneasy feeling that raising prices will alienate our client/friend, and this is an unhealthy attitude leading directly to business failure. Prices must be kept at levels that insure profit.

Face it—there is an element of truth to the supposition that you will probably lose a certain number of clients when you raise

Raise prices when necessary to a **profitable** level...not an **obscene** level!

prices. Those that leave as a result leave because of a perception that the price is unequal to the value received. That is all right, believe it or not. Haven't you yourself quit buying a product or service because you no longer felt it worth it? That is your consumer right, just as it is theirs. A funny thing happens, though. Those client/friends who left as a result of the price change are usually replaced by others who become your "friends" too. And this will continue as long as you raise prices when necessary. Consider this: If you are a stylist for forty years, do you honestly expect to retain the same clients for the entire period? Of course not! Clientele will change periodically for a host of reasons. Probably the best reason to lose certain clients is because of a price raise.

What will happen is that other clients will take their place—clients more willing to pay a higher tariff, and less likely to leave at the next raise. It is an odd fact that the higher the price of the services, the less clients leave because of raises. Upon reflection, this makes sense. Lower-priced salons attract clients chiefly because of their low prices. When prices are raised, that client has lost his or her main incentive to visit that salon and will then, in all probability, seek out another salon that meets his or her perceived needs. As the salon becomes more expensive, fewer and fewer clients are attracted by price alone, and the subsequent raising of prices has less effect on their leaving. At the high end of the pricing spectrum, very few clients leave because of a price hike. The closer to the bottom pricing levels one gets, the more likely clients are to leave over prices. This means that with every price increase the salon eliminates more and more clients who will leave because of a higher price.

Although difficult for some to accept, you must divorce friendship from business. This type of "friendship" is not really a friendship anyway, being a one-sided relationship (what can *you* give *me*!), and is not respectful of your professionalism and your right to earn a living at that profession. I dare say most clients who leave because of a price raise do not turn down salary raises in their own fields!

Many a salon has had to close its doors for no other reason than a well-meaning and sensitive owner failing to raise service prices when necessary, due to a misguided desire to salve client displeasure…which may have never materialized at all!

FORMULA TO RAISE PRICES ON

Here is a formula to base price raises on:

To determine the percentage that costs have increased from one year to the next, you will need the following formula:

Last Year	= LY
Current Year	= CY
Variance	= V
Percentage Change	= %C

To calculate an increase in cost from one year to the next in a percentage, you will need the following formula:

$$V = LY - CY$$
$$\%C = V / LY$$

EXAMPLE

1993 Cost of labor was	$10,000
1992 Cost of labor was	$ 7,500
Labor increased	$ 2,500

V	=	$10,000 – 7,500
V	=	$ 2,500
%C	=	$ 2,500 / $7,500
%C	=	33%

Prices should therefore be increased 33% to retain the same profit status as before:

EXAMPLE

Sales Price (Old)	= SPO	$30.00
Percentage Change	= %C	33%
Sales Price (New)	= SPN	

SPN =	SPO + (SPO × %C)	
SPN =	$30.00 + ($30.00 × 33%)	
SPN =	$30.00 + ($9.99)	
SPN =	$39.99	

STAFF PRICES

What each stylist in your employ charges for services is an area you should carefully study. It is common in many salons to set up a pricing structure that is the same for everyone in the salon. This may be counterproductive and lead to an environment where some stylists are extremely busy and others do a lot of sitting. (And griping!)

The flaws in a uniform pricing structure for all staff members are several. First, it puts an unfair burden on the junior stylist to try to perform at a level of another, more-talented or knowledge-able coworker. In a salon where everyone charges the same for each service, what usually happens is that several stylists have a healthy clientele (the stylists who have been there longer and/or exhibit more ability), some have a moderate amount of clients (stylists with less seniority and/or talent), and some have virtually no clientele (the newer members of the staff). This is where the myth that it takes "a year or two to build a clientele" comes from. It certainly does, under these type of conditions!

Something else happens in a pricing situation such as this. The more-junior and less-busy stylists tend to do a bit of fabricating about their experience and ability to potential clients. They hope they will be believed and succeed in convincing that client to sit in their chairs. This, however, is a tactic doomed to failure. For one thing, people, especially those clients who have been visiting the salon for a period, are not foolish enough to buy into what is an obvious misrepresentation.

This is a strategy that can backfire in embarrassing ways. I once observed a new stylist trying to convince a new client he had been styling hair for five years when in reality he was weeks out of school. After watching the young man struggle with her haircut for some minutes, the client dryly remarked, "You haven't learned much in five years, have you?"

And, a salon that sets the same price for all the stylists (unless it is a very small salon with everyone of comparable ability) is not being fair to the person on the other side of the chair, as well. The client is asked to pay the same price as she would for the services of a more experienced, more talented veteran. Of course, there will not be many who will, again leading to the empty-chair syndrome.

There is a better way to avoid all this, by using a "level system" which we will touch upon, shortly.

By and large, it is not fair to expect a stylist to perform at a level he or she is not yet ready for and, by the same token, it is not fair to the client to pay top fees for a lower-quality service that she could obtain from another stylist in the same salon at the same price. Although the salon owner may claim that all the stylists in the salon are the same, the people coming in the door will know differently and if they are expected to pay the same price for services of widely diverse quality, they will opt for the stylist they perceive to give the best value for that price.

There are several ways out of this dilemma; the best we have found is the utilization of a "level system." In such a system, levels are created based on the quality of work performed. Stylists in each level have a clearly defined body of criteria necessary to achieve that level, and, just as importantly, are provided with the means to achieve the next-higher level if they will work hard and apply themselves. Each level, of course, has a different pricing structure.

In our own salon, we use a three-tiered level system, which we call Codesigner, Designer and Senior Designer. It is not easy to be promoted to the next level—it requires a lot of study and hard work to achieve that goal—but the sense of accomplishment and the resulting rewards are worth it. We also make certain that the salon's clientele is aware of what it takes to get to each level, and when a stylist is promoted, most of his or her clients feel they have shared in the accomplishment and most remain with the newly promoted stylist, gladly paying the increased fees. They know promotion is not freely given, but hard earned, and they respect what the stylist has achieved.

A bonus to the salon owner using such a system is the boost in staff morale. Stylists in such a salon realize that they are involved in a career, not just a job, and the steps that they are required to take are adding to their professionalism, increasing their value both intrinsically and in a very real, monetary sense. A newspaper congratulatory ad is run upon each promotion, "big-dealizing" the event, and a formal announcement is mailed to the stylist's clients. We don't see it as a small thing and we don't treat it as a small thing.

Always remember—you train your competition!

Staff Pricing Formula

The staff pricing in a level system can be derived with similar formulas to those used in the initial discussion. Multiply labor costs by 3 to 3.5, and again, use the reverse of this to determine employee cost.

CHAPTER EIGHT

Adding or Deleting Products and Services

The decision to add or delete products and services is relatively simple. Such decisions should be based on the financial formula previously stated, and as follows:

1/3 of the service income pays for overhead it creates.

1/3 of the service income pays for the labor used to provide the service.

1/3 of the service income goes to the owner as profit.

If the service is not meeting this formula, it must be evaluated as to its merits. The service could possibly be a leader in providing other services or sales, and if so, this could be a reason for retaining it. Otherwise it should be dropped from your program. Keep in mind that you need to determine if the other services or sales such a loss leader provides are profitable enough to justify taking a loss on that service.

Adding or deleting products is a decision based simply on the answer to the question, "Does the particular product 'turn over' fast enough to produce cash flow?" If not, it is time to evaluate and probably eliminate it.

There is no room for sentiment here. If the service doesn't meet the above formula, and doesn't provide sufficient profit as a loss leader, it should be dropped like a hot potato, unless you can figure out a way to allow it to meet the formula, perhaps by raising the price sufficiently, changing the labor costs, or other such means.

Years ago, for example, commissions paid to stylists were as high as 75—80%. Today, if any such pay schemes exist, which is doubtful, the salon is losing money on its stylists' efforts, and if

Does the product turn over fast enough to produce sufficient cash flow?

the salon manages to keep its doors open, it is usually only because the owner is sacrificing his or her labor and income.

In today's business climate, commissions or pay scales allowing the person performing the service (stylist or technician) to receive a higher rate than one-third of the gross price charged are unsound, unless the overhead cost of the service is reduced accordingly, in proportion to whatever is paid above 33%. Or, the difference must come from the profit "third." As owners found out two and three decades ago, commissions of 75% were disastrous. To expect to provide for overhead and provide a profit from the remaining 25% was impossible. Those who lowered commission rates and/or pay scales survived; those who didn't closed their doors or held on by their fingernails, sacrificing their own income to pay exorbitant salaries.

As much as we'd like to be "good guys," it is *never* the function of a business to provide jobs. The sole reason for a business to exist is to provide a reasonable profit for the owner(s). If this doesn't happen, because of poor management practices, then the enterprise cannot qualify as a business, but more accurately fits the description of a "hobby" or a charitable enterprise. Unfortunately it won't meet the government's standards for a charity and won't qualify for a different tax status!

What is usually the case in salons that pay unprofitable commissions to their stylists, or base their pay scales on schemes that deny a profit to the salon, is that their service fees are simply too low to provide a reasonable profit. The fact that there are many, many salons in existence that operate in this manner doesn't justify the practice. It is undeniably unbusinesslike and unprofessional. Virtually no other trade or profession operates in such a manner. Can anyone imagine an accountant, a dentist, a lawyer, a doctor or for that matter any professional that operates a business by plowing all its income back into salaries for its employees and denying the business a profit? Any business that would do so would be marginal at best and would not face a lengthy future.

That is the sad state of many hair salons, an intolerable condition for any other trade, but one that continues to exist in ours.

An all-too-common scene is this: A salon, with a base price of $20 per haircut, employs four stylists in addition to the owner.

The average yearly gross of each stylist is $40,000, while the owner takes in $60,000. She pays herself a salary of $500 per week. The total service dollars annually grossed is $220,000. Each stylist is paid a commission of 55% of their weekly gross for an annual wage of $22,000. The cost (to the owner) of that service—let's be charitable—runs 35% or $14,000 per stylist. This leaves a profit, per stylist, of 10%, or $4,000—hardly a significant return on investment.

And, this is only if everything runs perfectly smoothly. It doesn't provide for the losses incurred in training new stylists, or losses suffered when a producing stylist decides to open her own salon four blocks away and takes her clientele with her. It doesn't provide for illnesses and accidents that result in lack of production, or for the employee you terminated six months ago filing for unemployment insurance which you must pay. It doesn't provide for these and a hundred other exigencies that can and do occur.

Also, from the slim returns, you as owner are expected to remodel, advertise and promote, provide for future expenses and emergencies, and in dozens of other ways grow your business! A one-third profit provides for all these things; anything less cannot. Such a business, on the surface, appears to be healthy, but it is on the constant verge of bankruptcy and insolvency.

The answer, obviously, is to raise service fees to a profitable level. The problem is, the raise that would be necessary would result in a dramatic loss of business and be counterproductive. A real dilemma is posed.

The owner of a business in this situation must make some hard choices. She can continue to operate the salon as before with the knowledge that she is providing jobs to stylists at the detriment of a healthy bottom line—she is in effect husbanding a sick animal—or she can take steps that will make it healthy. To cure a sick tree, a good pruning is sometimes the only answer.

The best and quickest way to make it healthy is to lower commissions to the proper level, whatever level would be needed to provide a reasonable profit to the business. Of course, by doing so, the owner will lose employees as their income will drop precipitously. The result would be to reduce the gross, but increase the net to a reasonable level. Then, as business increases, the owner needs to add new stylists who are better qualified to increase their gross. A price raise initiated at the same time that commissions are lowered would be advisable. The reason the commissions (in our example) were too high in the first place is that prices were too low to provide a sufficient income for employees at the proper commission. Therefore, prices need to be adjusted upward until they reach the proper levels and then they need to be watched carefully to reflect factors such as inflation.

This appears cold-hearted and may well be, but the truth of the matter is that far too many salons have operated in an unbusinesslike fashion for years, and have contributed to the unprofessionalism and unprofitability of the salon business.

It has been said, very accurately, that 20% of all stylists and salons enjoy 80% of the business and the remaining 80% of stylists fight over the remaining 20%. In no other trade is this true. For years, the industry has hidden its head in the sand over this, and refused to face the facts. The result is a profession that demands little respect from others. How can we expect others to respect us when we conduct our business in this manner? Ignoring the situation won't make it go away, nor will it solve it. Only by dispassionately looking at the facts and making the right choices can hairstylists ever universally enjoy the prestige and income of other trades and professions.

In what other field can it be said that only two out of five graduates still are employed in that field two years after receiving their license? This is reprehensible and is a state that only exists in the hairstyling industry. There is not another trade or profession that would tolerate a situation such as this. Can anyone even comprehend a scenario in which only 40% of accountants still worked in that field only two years after receiving their degrees? Or computer programmers, or police officers, or teachers, or salespersons? One cannot name a comparable situation in any other field.

The chief reason is that too many salons don't operate their businesses as a business should be operated. The only way to ever remedy the situation is to get prices and commissions and pay scales to the place where they provide a reasonable profit. The myth continually perpetuated is that the answer is to "educate the stylist" to where she is technically more qualified, "knows more cuts and performs them better," etc. Well, the United States has a better-trained styling community than virtually anyplace else in the world, but one of the lowest per capita incomes when compared to other countries. The answer is not in more and more technical excellence—most stylists use but a handful of the many styles they have mastered the majority of the time, and a booming business can and has been built and sustained with a limited repertoire—but in more solid education in sound business principles. This is not to say that technical artistry should be ignored, but hand-in-hand with it should be the teaching of basic business economics.

Salon owners need to get their house in order if they expect to prosper and not merely survive.

CHAPTER NINE

Banking Services and Accounts

Next to your accountant, your most important business partner should be your bank. Before you got into business for yourself, if you are like most of us, you used banks for fairly basic needs. A checking and savings account, perhaps application for various loans, and that was about the extent of it.

For the business owner, banks and similar financial institutions offer many more services. Sound business advice can be obtained, as well as referral to other organizations and individuals who provide guidance and advice for the growth of your salon.

Next to your accountant, your most important business partner is your bank (and your banker!).

Each bank, as well, usually offers a multitude of other services, including various types of checking and savings accounts better suited to your needs than the accounts you were used to as an individual. These accounts are governed by the bank's creativity and also by the rules imposed upon them by state and federal authorities and the parent institution.

For instance, the owner of a personal checking account usually isn't entitled to interest on the money in the account. This represents a loss of income when you consider that the same sum, invested in an interest-bearing instrument, would be earning interest or dividends. With a business checking account, higher sums are usually at stake. This type of account can represent a significant loss in income over a period of time.

For this reason, many financial institutions offer "Sweep" or "Cash Management Account" (CMA) checking accounts. They are available to individual as well as corporate businesses, and pay interest on the money in the account.

In a CMA account, there exist two accounts. One account is used to write checks, while the other account is used as an investment account. Periodically, money is "swept," or transferred, from the check writing account to the investment account. The amount swept is usually an amount that will leave the check writing account at a predetermined balance.

For example, you have determined that there will exist in your check writing account a balance of $5,000. The financial institution would then "sweep" your account balance automatically to maintain a $5,000 balance in your check-writing account. The investment account will then earn a rate of interest. As you write checks, amounts will be transferred from the investment account to the check-writing account to cover the checks. Service fees are usually assessed on the check-writing account in accordance with minimum balances (usually $1,500), while interest is earned on the investment accounts average daily balance.

The financial institution will help you determine the amounts needed in both accounts to enable you to know how much money you need to avoid service charges.

WORKING THE "FLOAT"

Another financial tool commonly used by big business and available to any size enterprise, but surprisingly oftentimes not used by salon owners, is the practice of "working the float."

Using, or working, the float simply amounts to obtaining a short-term, interest-free loan. Most accounts payable (bills) provide a "grace period" at the end of which the amount owed must be paid. Commonly, this is a thirty-day period, but sometimes it will be as long as sixty days, ninety days, or even longer. If you take advantage of the grace period, you not only obtain the use of the product or whatever the purchase consisted of, but you also have the use of the money owed for other purposes. Many times, it is to your advantage to work the float, although not always.

As an example, you buy six dozen perms and the dealer offers two paying options—to pay cash on delivery or to pay the same amount in thirty days without penalty, interest, or extra charge. In a case such as this, the astute salon owner would opt to pay at the last possible moment, thereby freeing up the amount of the purchase for other uses.

If there is an incentive for paying promptly, say, the distributor will deduct 1 1/2% from the bill, then you must determine if it would more beneficial to pay early and receive the discount or to use the money for something else. You would need to determine if you would realize more savings from investing that sum in another investment vehicle or purchase, or by taking advantage of the discount, and then decide accordingly.

There is an important economic dynamic at work when you delay payment, and that is inflation. In our system of economics, some amount of inflation is inevitable and will be greater or smaller depending on a host of other factors. One thing is for certain: Even in times we claim are "inflation-free" there is always some eroding of the value of our basic dollar unit. It is a safe assumption then, that the dollar you hold in your hand today is not going to be worth as much (in purchasing power) as it will in even as short a period as one to three months.

This means that the value of the purchase you made a month ago has probably risen while the dollars you pay for it are worth less. By using that sum properly, either by investing in an instrument such as an interest-bearing checking account that earns money, or by making another purchase (also beating the inflation factor), you are now working the float properly and to your advantage.

If you simply sit on the money, doing nothing, you have defeated the purpose, gained nothing, and probably lost money. This is where a CMA account is particularly valuable. Don't just let the money sit, not earning interest or at least being utilized for other payables that will reduce an interest load. With inactivity, you have misused an interest-free loan, and the bad news is that you will still have the bill to pay! Keep in mind that money is a commodity, just as a bottle of shampoo is, and that it should be working for you, not sitting idle or being wasted on foolish purchases. Money, used properly, can create additional wealth.

It used to be easy for a small business to set up an interest-bearing checking account, but many states (including our own of Indiana) have made them illegal (just another instance of our friendly government's helping hand to the small businessman or -woman!). However, like many obstacles, this can also be often overcome. Each state is different, so consult with your accountant as to your own options. In our state, we can legally create an account that accomplishes the same thing by setting up accounts that "roll over," another form of a CMA account.

Don't worry needlessly that by taking advantage of the float you are somehow doing something illegal or unethical. It is simply a good and accepted business practice to do so, and one practiced universally by big business and astute businesses of all sizes. Ask your distributors if they use the float with their own accounts payable, and if they are forthright, they will assure you that they do.

If you think the amounts concerned are too negligible to worry about—a $50-phone bill here, a $200-perm bill there, four trade show tickets over there—think about this: If you added up all such bills with at least a thirty-day grace period over the course of an entire year, it might come, to, say, $10,000. If you had taken advantage of the float for all of them, what you would have gained would be the equivalent of an interest-free loan of $10,000 for thirty days! Try going to your bank for the same loan with equivalent terms!

As a final word on the subject, when working the float always make sure the bill is paid before the grace period is up. You can (and should) go to the absolute last possible minute before submitting your payment, but don't go beyond that point and end up paying penalties and/or interest or you will not only have defeated the purpose but will in all likelihood end up losing money.

CHAPTER TEN

Equipment—Purchasing, Remodeling and Replacing

If you are in business long enough (and hopefully, you will be!), there will come a point when equipment will need to be replaced. All equipment wears out. Therefore, you should begin now to set aside savings to pay for equipment upgrades.

Equipment purchases should rarely be made from cash flow monies.

This is an important-enough rule to be isolated and set in bold type!

Equipment should be purchased with borrowed money or savings. Cash flow monies are reserved for short-term needs—paying bills, financing inventory, or accounts receivable.

Equipment expenditures are an important budget category. Salon owners should set up within their budget a category for capital expenditures which will set aside funds today to provide for their equipment needs in the future. The owner also needs to understand the borrowing costs associated with a timed purchase. The interest cost incurred in a timed purchase should be an item that is included in the budget, as that is a cost of doing business.

Not having the use of a particular piece of equipment could cost you money. It is recommended that if you buy multiple pieces of the same kind of equipment, they should be purchased from the same vendor so that replacement parts can be used from dormant units. This is especially sound advice if repairs are frequent or expensive, or if the service department from your vendor is slow in responding to your needs.

Here is a tax tip that can help you better plan equipment purchases: If you have an item of equipment that has been completely written off through depreciation, consider trading the unit for a new unit. This will avoid the gain from any sale as trade-ins are not a taxable transaction. You may not receive as much in a trade as in a sale, but consider the tax effect of reporting the gain on the sale before ruling out a trade. Your accountant can provide this information.

The inverse is true if the equipment has not yet been depreciated. Equipment in this situation should be sold—not traded—thereby incurring a loss in the current year of the sale of equipment that would otherwise be spread out over several years in a trade, and therefore a better tax advantage.

Equipment should always be evaluated according to the financial benefit it will bring to the business.

For instance, let's say you have been maintaining your accounting system by pencil and paper, and you are contemplating purchasing a computer with an accounting program. You estimate you now spend an average of six hours per week "running the numbers" manually, and a computer program will reduce that to two hours. If you know that spending the same amount of time cutting hair will return $50 per hour in gross wages, and $30 in net wages, and if you know also that a complete computer system, hardware and program, will set you back $2,000, you will recoup the investment in 66.6 hours ($2000 ÷ $30 = 66.6). At four additional cutting hours per week (the hours gained), it would take approximately 16 1/2 weeks to recoup the investment.

If there were finance charges associated with the purchase, this would need to be figured in as well.

On something like this, it is relatively easy to figure the financial benefit to the salon. On other items, it may be more difficult, such as a decision to remodel. Remodeling expenses are one item that will definitely benefit from being budgeted early.

You may decide that it would be advisable to do major remodeling on a fixed periodic basis. You would look over your depreciation schedule and determine the best time, tax-wise, to trade or sell major used equipment and purchase new. Figuring as best you can what the general cost will be, taking into account expected inflation and other variables, you can arrive at least at a ballpark figure, which you can then add as an item to your budget, planning for it in advance. Then, when the time comes, you should be

close to having all the necessary funds in hand to complete the job, and should not have to dip into cash flow monies or providing financing from deleterious interest rates.

It would be advisable to have a contingency account set up and provided for in your budget for emergency equipment purchases—for example when a styling chair breaks down unexpectedly or a shampoo sink develops a crack and can no longer be used.

No one can predict all the times when new equipment will need to be purchased, but if such decisions are systematically planned for in advance, then the crises will be much fewer and farther between.

CHAPTER ELEVEN

Computers

Not long ago, a computer was considered a luxury tool affordable by only the most affluent salons. Today, becoming computerized is fast becoming a necessity to remain competitive, as essential in today's salon as the styling chairs and sinks. True, there will probably be salons—and successful ones at that—ten years from now that still won't be computerized, but why start out at bat with two strikes against you?

It's a computer world, like it or not, and the salon owner who recognizes that fact of life and accepts it, will be farther ahead than the one who resists.

As products change almost daily, this is not the place to rate different hardware and software systems. Basically, as of this writing, the minimum we would advise in a new system is a 486-megabyte (MB) hard drive with at least 4 MB of RAM (8 is preferable), and a hard drive of at least 150 MB. Operating systems are undergoing changes, but either DOS or Windows would probably be the best as most software packages run on these. MacIntosh users would argue, and it appears more and more software manufacturers are producing products for Macs, but there still doesn't appear to be as much available at this time. Keep in mind this could change and probably will.

The best bet is to talk to someone you consider knowledgeable and ask what they recommend.

Likewise, for software—products change so quickly any recommendations soon become obsolete—consult a knowledgeable expert for what they advise, based on your needs.

Most software should be tried before it is purchased. If the manufacturer doesn't provide a test package, look around for salons that have the system you are considering and see if they will let you give it a good look to determine if it is the system for your particular needs.

Does your computer vendor have a good reputation for service?

Look to see what support is provided and at what cost. Does the manufacturer provide training in the system and how extensive is that training? Or are you expected to master it on your own, an arduous feat sometimes, especially if you are completely unfamiliar with computers and programs? Most manufacturers of systems claim their software is "user-friendly" but that is a totally subjective judgment, and the best way to find out if this claim is true is by using it for a trial period.

It is safe to say there is virtually no area in salon life that cannot be made easier and more productive than through the intelligent use of computers. There are programs that will handle inventory, bookkeeping and accounting, appointments, payroll, training and education, salon design, retailing, personnel management, marketing and advertising, mailings, taxes, financial reports, forecasting and goal-setting, agendas, time management, and dozens of other tasks. You can even obtain programs that will market your salon over the phone when you are sitting at home in front of the fireplace!

Computers today are extremely user-friendly!

Those of you who are computer-illiterate, don't feel bad. Each of us was in the same boat at one time. Although computers are capable of more and more complex functions, they are becoming more and more user-friendly!

First, there are five basic components. These are the **hardware** (containing four of the components: the **computer** itself, the **keyboard**, the **screen**, and a **printer**), and a **software program.**

The computer itself contains a hard drive or floppy disks or both. Don't even consider a computer without a hard drive (some of the older ones you might get cheap), and get the biggest hard drive you can afford. Computers that must run on floppy drives are not only too inconvenient, but they don't have enough storage capacity for multiple applications. There aren't any programs designed for the salon anymore that will run on a floppy-disk computer—they all require a hard drive.

The size of main memory is very important. There must be enough to support the program(s) and store the information you want to record. Minimum requirements for today's uses are at least 650K RAM (main memory) and at least a 100MB hard disk.

Most colleges offer basic computer classes to beginners and many retail outlets do as well, at a minimum price.

As in other equipment purchases, paying cash or setting up payment programs may not be as fiscally wise as investigating the benefits of leasing. Many times you can get a whole lot more for your computer dollar by leasing, paying for today's use with inflated dollars tomorrow, and in addition realizing a substantial offset in taxes. Refer to Chapter Ten on Equipment—Purchasing, Remodeling, and Replacing for ideas on how to finance.

Ask a dealer who is familiar with your kind of business about what system to purchase.

CHAPTER TWELVE

Profit-Sharing

Profit-sharing retirement plans allow the employer to fund and deduct contributions paid to his or her retirement account. However, the employer must contribute to the employee's plan in the same percentages the employer has contributed to his or her own. The rules become very complicated and should be tailored to your individual situation; therefore, a discussion of this matter is better served through the advice of your accountant, one-on-one. However, we will present our opinion as to the aspect of profit-sharing plans overall.

Profit-sharing plans are those that allow the employer to deduct, for income tax purposes, the contribution made on the employees' behalf. The employee does not pay income tax currently on the contribution until such time that he or she withdraws the money from the plan (which is not until the age of 59 1/2, to avoid penalties). The money contributed on the employees' behalf is usually calculated on a percentage of the gross payroll.

For example, if the owner of the salon was to contribute for the employee 15% of his or her wages and the employee's gross pay was $10,000 per year, the contribution would be $1,500 ($10,000 × 15%).

Most employees are young people. They are starting life in the real world and are therefore looking for benefits they can currently use. Profit-sharing plans unfortunately do not provide this benefit. The $1,500 in the example above is "locked" in a retirement plan that the employee can withdraw only at a cost that is more than if the benefits were paid as a wage.

Secondly, the contribution costs the employer $1,500 more for the benefit of having this employee. The employer cannot be discretionary in his or her ability to provide this benefit. It has to be given to all employees. Certain restrictions can apply (for in-

Profit-sharing plans can be complicated to compute and, in general, are not recommended for most salons.

stance there could be a two-year waiting period in some circumstances) but the point is clear—you may not want to give the money to certain employees but you must, by law. We do not know of many who like to be told how they should spend their hard-earned money, and in this case it can be avoided.

If retirement plans are something you want to provide, perhaps a better way is to give the employees a bonus and let them use that money to fund an Individual Retirement Account (IRA). Bonuses are discretionary and therefore you can reward individual employees as you see fit, according to merit. This, we feel is a better method in most cases than profit-sharing plans, which, in general, we don't think work to the advantage of most salons, although your own case may be different. Your accountant is the best source of advice if you are considering this option.

CHAPTER THIRTEEN

Profit & Loss Statements and Other Reports

Profit and loss statements are only one of the reports a salon should monitor on no less than a monthly basis. These reports include:

1. Income statements

2. Balance sheet

3. Cash flow statement

INCOME STATEMENT

This statement tells the user how much your business has generated in cash inflows versus how much the company has spent through cash outflows. This is the **operating statement** of the company. Inflows are representative of services and sales that are provided by the company—the reason you are in business.

Outflows are the money it takes in order to earn the inflow. We all know it takes money to make money. Our goal is to make more than we spend. The Income Statement is the driving statement of your company. It is from this statement that you can conclude if you are charging enough, if you are spending too much in any one category, etc. The real purpose of this statement comes to life when a few analyses are performed.

The first is **common size analysis**. This analysis enables the user to determine how much gross income is being used by a particular outflow. The income statement is broken down into its components with total gross income being the denominator and all other accounts balances in the income statement being the numerator.

For example, if you wanted to know how much of your sales dollar is being used to pay your advertising, the formula would be:

Advertising = $ 1,000 or 3%

Gross Sales = $30,000

Your conclusion is that 3% of every sales dollar is being used to pay for advertising bills. This analysis by itself is not very meaningful, however, if you develop a trend over the years, unless you have access to industry standards when the information becomes quite useful. Many computer software programs calculate common size reports as standard reports. See the worksheet at the end of this chapter.

The second analysis is **variance**. Income and expenses for the same period are subtracted to determine the increase or decrease in the reported period of time. This analysis is extremely useful in determining what effect, if any, an increase or decrease in expense had on income.

In addition, this analysis is very useful in determining how profits increased or decreased from prior periods. An additional analysis would include the calculation of a percentage variance. This is the same analysis as the variance divided by the base period. This will help you determine how much a particular income or expense category increased or decreased on a percentage basis. This is useful in evaluating known market fluctuations and will provide you with a gauge of your own performance. Again, see the worksheet at the end of the chapter.

The final analysis is the **budget analysis**. This would include the variance analysis as well as total budget usage. This report tells you if you are in line with the plan you have developed for your salon. The differences are not always bad—they *are* accounts that require investigation. If you are to reach your goal you must monitor your progress. Again, see the worksheet at the end of the chapter.

BALANCE SHEET

This statement indicates what you own, who you owe, and how much you have invested into the company. A **balance sheet**, unlike the income statement, is a "picture-in-time." The income statement is a flow; it represents a period. A balance sheet is important because it tracks the fruits of your efforts and tells you what you have to show for your hard work.

The balance sheet will tell how much you own and how much you owe. It shows how much money you have retained in the salon and how much you have invested. It shows who owns the assets, as well as what is owed the creditors and how much the owner has invested. The balance sheet gives statement users at any point in time the answers to these questions. It is vital information for bank loan officers and future investors.

CASH FLOW STATEMENT

This is the most important statement in your arsenal. Unfortunately, an untrained individual cannot develop this statement without the aid of a computer program or a professional to give them guidance. This statement combines the information of the income statement with that of the balance sheet to tell the owner how his or her profits were spent. The age-old question is, "I had profits, but where did they go?" Some computer programs provide some kind of cash flow analysis, but it would not hurt to seek the advice of an accountant to help you to provide a template for developing a cash flow statement.

WORKSHEETS

COMMON SIZE ANALYSIS		
	Dollars	Common Size Percent
Gross Sales and Service		
Sales:		
Sales—Hair Products Direct	$ 150,000	60.00%
Sales—Hair Accessories	30,000	12.00%
Sales—Other	10,000	4.00%
Total Sales	190,000	76.00%

Common Size Analysis (cont.)

	Dollars	Common Size Percent
Services:		
Service Income—Haircuts	$ 20,000	8.00%
Service Income—Styling	30,000	12.00%
Service Income—Other	10,000	4.00%
Total Service Income	$ 60,000	24.00%
Total Gross Income	$ 250,000	100.00%
Cost of Sales		
Beginning Inventory	$ 100,000	40.00%
Purchases	75,000	30.00%
Less Ending Inventory	(105,000)	–42.00%
Total Cost of Sales	$ 70,000	28.00%
Gross Margin	$ 180,000	72.00%
Operating Expenses:		
Labor		
Wages—Gross	$ 20,000	8.00%
Payroll Tax Expense	2,300	0.92%
Employee Benefits	2,000	0.80%
Continuing Education	1,000	0.40%
Total Labor	$ 25,300	10.12%
Operating Supplies	$ 15,000	6.00%
Advertising		
Newspaper	$ 1,300	0.52%
Radio	1,400	0.56%
Television	1,500	0.60%
Printing	500	0.20%
Total Advertising	$ 4,700	1.88%
Small Tools	$ 3,000	1.20%
Utilities		
Water	$ 9,000	3.60%
Electricity	5,000	2.00%
Gas	1,000	0.40%
Refuse	400	0.16%
Total Utilities	$ 15,400	6.16%
Office Supplies		
Cleaning Supplies	$ 1,000	0.40%
Postage	500	0.20%
Repairs		
Equipment	1,500	0.60%
Building	500	0.20%
Total Repairs	$ 2,000	0.80%

Common Size Analysis (cont.)

	Dollars	Common Size Percent
Travel Expense		
Reimbursement	$ 1,000	0.40%
Gas, Grease, Oil	1,000	0.40%
Motels	700	0.28%
Meals	300	0.12%
Total Travel	$ 3,000	1.20%
Entertainment	$ 750	0.30%
Insurance		
Liability	$ 2,500	1.00%
Professional	2,500	0.80%
Auto	500	0.20%
Total Insurance	$ 5,000	2.00%
Property Taxes	$ 250	0.10%
Dues and Memberships	700	0.28%
Depreciation—Equipment	2,000	0.80%
Rent Expense		
Equipment	100	0.04%
Building	12,000	4.80%
Total Rent Expense	$ 12,100	4.84%
Cash Over and Short	$ 500	0.20%
Bank Service Fee	2,500	1.00%
Interest Expense	5,000	2.00%
Telephone		
Local	650	0.26%
Long Distance	360	0.14%
Advertising	750	0.30%
Cellular	1,000	0.40%
Total Telephone	$ 2,760	1.10%
Total Expenses	$ 101,460	40.58%
Net Income before taxes	$ 78,540	31.42%
Taxes		
Federal Income Tax	$ (11,781)	−4.71%
State Income Tax	(6,205)	−2.48%
Total Tax	(17,986)	−7.19%
Net Income Tax	$ 96,526	38.61%

VARIANCE ANALYSIS—ACTUAL

	Actual Dollars 1994	1993	Dollars Variance	Percent Variance
Gross Sales and Service				
Sales:				
Sales—Hair Products Direct	$150,000	130,000	20,000	15.385%
Sales—Hair Accessories	30,000	25,000	5,000	20.000%
Sales—Other	10,000	7,500	2,500	33.333%
Total Sales	$190,000	162,500	27,500	16.923%
Services:				
Service Income—Haircuts	$ 20,000	25,000	(5,000)	−20.000%
Service Income—Styling	30,000	35,000	(5,000)	−14.286%
Service Income—Other	10,000	8,000	2,000	25.000%
Total Service Income	$ 60,000	68,000	(8,000)	−11.765%
Total Gross Income	$250,000	230,500	19,500	8.460%
Cost of Sales				
Beginning Inventory	$100,000	98,000	2,000	2.041%
Purchases	75,000	70,000	5,000	7.143%
Less Ending Inventory	(105,000)	(100,000)	(5,000)	5.000%
Total Cost of Sales	$ 70,000	68,000	2,000	2.941%
Gross Margin	$180,000	162,500	17,500	10.769%
Operating Expenses:				
Labor				
Wages—Gross	$ 20,000	25,000	(5,000)	−20.000%
Payroll Tax Expense	2,300	2,875	(575)	−20.000%
Employee Benefits	2,000	2,500	(500)	−20.000%
Continuing Education	1,000	750	250	33.333%
Total Labor	$ 25,300	31,125	(5,825)	−18.715%
Operating Supplies	15,000	14,975	25	0.167%
Advertising				
Newspaper	1,300	1,350	(50)	−3.704%
Radio	1,400	1,000	400	40.000%
Television	1,500	100	1,400	1400.000%
Printing	500	1,000	(500)	−50.000%
Total Advertising	$ 4,700	3,450	1,250	36.232%
Small Tools	3,000	4,000	(1,000)	−25.000%
Utilities				
Water	9,000	8,500	500	5.882%
Electricity	5,000	4,500	500	11.111%
Gas	1,000	800	200	25.000%
Refuse	400	400	0	0.000%
Total Utilities	$ 15,400	14,200	1,200	8.451%

VARIANCE ANALYSIS—BUDGET

	Dollars 1994	*Dollars 1993*	*Dollars Variance*
Office Supplies			
Cleaning Supplies	$ 1,000	1,500	(500)
Postage	500	500	0
Repairs			
Equipment	1,500	1,500	0
Building	500	200	300
Total Repairs	$ 2,000	1,700	300
Travel Expense			
Reimbursement	1,000	1,000	0
Gas, Grease, Oil	1,000	1,000	0
Motels	700	800	(100)
Meals	300	350	(50)
Total Travel	$ 3,000	3,150	(150)
Entertainment	750	1,000	(250)
Insurance			
Liability	2,500	2,500	0
Professional	2,000	2,000	0
Auto	500	500	0
Total Insurance	$ 5,000	5,000	0
Property Taxes	250	250	0
Dues and Memberships	700	800	(100)
Depreciation—Equipment	2,000	2,000	0
Rent Expense			
Equipment	100	100	0
Building	12,000	12,000	0
Total Rent Expense	$ 12,100	12,100	0
Cash Over and Short	500	500	0
Bank Service Fee	2,500	2,450	50
Interest Expense	5,000	5,000	0
Telephone			
Local	650	750	(100)
Long Distance	360	360	0
Advertising	750	750	0
Cellular	1,000	1,000	0
Total Telephone	$ 2,760	2,860	(100)
Total Expenses	$101,460	101,773	(313)
Net Income before taxes	$ 78,540	71,728	6,813
Taxes			
Federal Income Tax	(11,781)	(10,759)	(1,022)
State Income Tax	(6,205)	(5,666)	(538)
Total Tax	(17,986)	(16,426)	(1,560)
Net Income Tax	$ 96,526	88,153	8,373

CHAPTER FOURTEEN

Tax Planning

Good tax planning takes care of itself. A good tax plan has as one of its tactics the payment of the least amount of tax as far into the future as possible—legally. Many times, individuals mistakenly believe their tax professional is doing an excellent job when they receive a large sum as a tax refund. This is actually extremely poor tax planning.

This is not the wisest way to plan taxes.

Educational needs for your children must be planned and provided for.

Financially, it is an unsound move to be in a situation where you are knowingly paying more in tax installments than you owe, with the goal of receiving a large refund for such overpayment. This allows the government the use (and resulting income) of your tax money. A good tax plan will pay the minimum installment required by law, provided it is in line with realistic projections of what your ultimate liability will be. Although not usually as bad as overpayment, gross underpayment can be detrimental as well. Underpayment can lead to "crisis" tax management.

The ideal situation is one where tax payments are in line with projected liabilities—neither too much nor too little—which results in the final payment of taxes being as close as possible to your projections.

Proper tax planning takes into account other facets as well. Things like providing for retirement or for your children's education need to be planned for as well.

Wise tax planning accomplishes many things. It can help provide capital for expansion. There are three recognized methods of tax planning: **transactional tax planning, strategic tax planning,** and **post-year-end tax planning** (perhaps more accurately known as "crisis management").

TRANSACTIONAL TAX PLANNING

This is a form of planning that concerns itself with the reduction of the tax consequence of a single event or series of events to its lowest total. As an example of this type of planning, let's say you are considering remodeling your waiting area by selling your chairs, couch, magazine racks, and coffee table and purchasing new furniture. In transactional planning, certain questions need to be answered before you do so. For instance, should the sale of the old furniture be reported on the installment basis? Is the old furniture depreciable or is it listed as an investment asset? What is your tax bracket this year compared to subsequent years (estimation)? Is the sale to a related party? These, and other, pertinent questions will help determine if selling the chairs is a wise move at the time.

STRATEGIC TAX PLANNING

This form of planning is an ongoing plan of when income should be recognized and when expenses ought to be paid. Normally, this is performed in the last months of the fiscal year, and the main objective is to receive income in the year in which it will benefit from the lowest tax rate and to pay out expenses in the year in which they will best offset the highest tax liability. Your accountant can best advise you on which technique you should use. Some techniques may involve prepayment of expenses or groupings of itemized deductions limited by percentages of adjusted gross income. To get the maximum efficiency out of strategic planning, you will have to estimate the current year's income as well as accurately predict future years' income. Again, working with a knowledgeable accountant who knows your business can give you a reasonably correct estimate.

POST-YEAR-END TAX PLANNING

Perhaps better known as "crisis management," this is descriptive of the kind of nonplanning that can get a salon into tax troubles. It is the response to poor or nonexistent planning and leads to nothing but woe!

It is the least effective method of tax planning since once a transaction has been consummated, most planning opportunities are gone. This method of "planning" leaves but few options, mainly limited to decisions on how much to invest in a SEP or IRA.

Also, tax laws change quickly, and further complicate the ability to effectively plan tax deferral or avoidance if you utilize this method. A sound tax planning program depends on working closely with a qualified accountant and investing that time in remaining current on tax law changes. As an owner, you need also to obtain a complete understanding of the effect of those laws on a selected tax-avoidance plan. Become a working partner with your tax advisor. If you are unfamiliar with tax planning, put in the time to become properly educated.

Tax planning involves annual planning for the timing of income and expenses. Business planning is determining the correct decision to make in questions such as whether or no to incorporate. You need to seek the advice of an individual who has the time and expertise to monitor current tax law changes. Income and Social Security/Medicare taxes can eat up to 45% of your company's profits, and is exactly why the services of a good accountant more than pay for themselves.

Be sure to have an understanding with your tax professional before you accept any advice, and keep in mind that *you* are ultimately responsible for your tax liability.

Sound tax planning has many advantages and few, if any, disadvantages. Proper planning can help provide necessary funds for future expansion, as well as show any potential lender you are in control of your business and are using sound practices in the way you manage it. This can tip a decision your way when requesting a loan.

It is proper tax planning that will tell you if and when you should change your business structure. Should your salon be incorporated, run as a sole proprietorship, or as a partnership? Your tax status greatly determines this decision.

As of this writing, taxes paid on income below $60,000 a year are less for a sole proprietor or partner than for a corporation. Above $60,000, the tax bite is lower for incorporated businesses. Please note that these figures are accurate only at the time this was written. As tax laws change rapidly, it is naturally best to check with your accountant and/or attorney for the best way to structure or restructure your own business.

And because the laws do change, it is advisable to periodically review your structure, in view of whatever current legislation is in force, to determine if perhaps a restructuring would not be advisable, to take the best advantage of the tax breaks available. Some years back, it was automatically assumed that incorporating was the best form of a business structure. No longer is that always the case. Indeed, many former small corporations, because of changes in tax codes, are restructuring into proprietorships. This could change again (and probably will) in the future as political regimes (and laws) change.

This means the only way to know which is the proper structure is to be aware and knowledgeable of the prevailing tax codes and laws, so that when you achieve a different economic position, you will be prepared to change the structure to take advantage.

CHAPTER FIFTEEN

Insurances

Providing proper insurance coverages for a salon is never a luxury. It is an absolute necessity. Only a very unwise person would operate under the kind of risks present to the uninsured, or, almost as bad, underinsured.

Basic coverages should include:

1. **Property coverage.** This is a form of term insurance that covers the owners investment in the physical property, including the building itself (if owned by the salon), and such items as styling chairs, shampoo sinks, waiting room furniture—in short, all the equipment and tools used in the operation of the salon. The retail product inventory needs to be included, and some also opt to provide money and securities coverage against robbery and burglary. A day or more of receipts can represent the loss of a healthy sum, if an armed robber decides to visit the salon for his own special brand of "payday"! It is not unknown that an employee is held up on her way to the bank to make a sizeable deposit. This risk can also be provided for.

2. **Liability coverage.** This is insurance on the salon owner's exposure to claims for personal injury or damage. Claims can range widely from someone slipping and falling on the carpet to someone suing because their hair turned bright green...when they were expecting blonde.

3. **Worker's Compensation Insurance.** Most, if not all, states require employers to carry Worker's Comp on their employees. Each state has different requirements, so heck with your local regulatory authorities or an insurance salesperson. Even in a booth rental situation, the owner of the salon may be responsible for providing Worker's Comp for

those he or she leases space to. Again, check state regulations. The safest way, in a booth rental situation, is for the owner to carry her own policy covering the booth renters and build that cost into the rental fee. This way, if someone misleads you into believing they have this insurance and don't, or fail to keep up payments, you will be covered.

Other coverages are:

1. **Nail services coverage.** If you offer nail services, be sure this is specifically covered in your liability package. Some packages cover this and some don't. If this is not men-

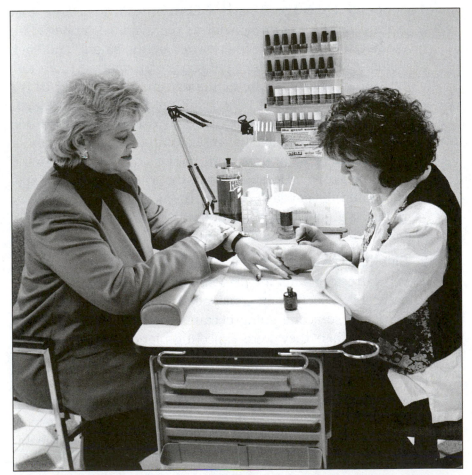

If you offer nail services, be sure this is specifically covered in your liability package.

tioned or is excluded, you should provide liability for these services.

2. **Tanning beds.** This takes a special policy, in most cases. Most insurance companies don't offer this package, so you will need to seek out the carrier that does. The best source of information on this is your tanning bed supplier.

3. **Business interruption insurance.** This provides against financial loss from temporary cessation of business due to factors such as the building burning down, a tornado, etc.

4. **Plate glass coverage.** Don't assume this is covered in your property coverage package. It needs to be listed separately. Even when you lease a building, most of the time the lease will require that you (the tenant) pay for plate glass damage, which can be expensive to say the least!

There is a general type of policy in the insurance industry commonly referred to as a B.O.P. or Business Owner's Policy. It covers most of the above insurances, at a generally lower cost than could be obtained by purchasing each coverage individually. Usually it is advisable to consult an independent agent for insurance needs, rather than a captive agent. An independent agency represents several different companies, while a captive agent or agency can only sell insurance from the single company they represent. The reason you should probably seek out an independent agency is obvious—they are able to get you better coverage at lower prices since they have access to many different lines and companies, unlike the captive agent who can only sell his or her company's policies. The captive agent's company may have the best deal on one or even several kinds of insurances, but it is unlikely they will have the best rate on all the insurances you need.

It may pay you to seek out an independent agency that specializes in salon coverages. They are around and can many times offer real savings. At the least, look for the agency that represents several insurance companies.

On liability coverages, the minimum coverage it is recommended that a salon carry is $500,000-combined single-limit, although it doesn't cost much more to go to $1 million, which is strongly advised. One million dollars in a lawsuit today is becoming small potatoes. A large salon operation would be well advised to consider taking out an Umbrella Policy which have a minimum limit of $1 million.

Other insurances which may be beneficial to consider are those insurances you can provide as employee benefits, such as group health, life, and disability policies. These can be paid in full by the employer or the employee can contribute in any amount or percentage up to 50% of the cost (the owner must provide a minimum of 50%), as determined by mutual agreement. Remember that you cannot have one employee paying one amount or percentage and another employee a different amount or percentage. All must be treated equally. There is no requirement, however, to provide for employee's dependents.

Providing group insurances as an employee benefit has another advantage for both parties, employee and employer. As each must contribute to the 7.65% FICA deduction, they both save if they agree that part of their salaries will be paid in the form of benefits. If the owner pays the entire cost of the employe's health insurance, for example, at a cost of say, $150 per month, and deducts half that amount from what he would have paid that person in salary, they both save the FICA contribution on the $75.

There are other insurances, such as Key Man Insurance, which, in the case of partnerships or where a salon has a key employee, provides funds in the event of that person's death to recover from the loss of her expertise and skill and income-production for the time it would take to replace what the person would have contributed. This is simply life insurance.

Life insurances are one of two types, term or whole life, or a combination of the two, referred to as "universal life." Term insurance pays simply the face value upon the death of the insured, while whole life does the same, although it also accrues cash values as the policy is maintained. Whole life policies are, therefore, more expensive than term contracts, and are not usually recommended, as the cash values accrue at a relatively low interest rate. If an individual took the equivalent in term insurance and took the difference in the premium paid between the two and invested in even a conservative interest-bearing instrument, such as a savings account, she would earn substantially more than the cash values the whole life policy would generate. The rationale that most who own (or sell) whole life policies use is that they represent a painless way to save. Indeed, for some, it is the *only* way they are able to save! But, financially, it is a poor investment. Universal life policies are somewhere in between, providing a combination of term and life. Again, the part of the premium that is applied to the whole life portion is generally a lousy investment. Years ago, a great deal of whole life insurance was sold to policy-holders and then people began wising up and it is suspected that universal life was, while not necessarily a "gimmick," at least an instrument invented to ease the strain (on insurance companies) of millions of people converting whole life into term. What it boils down to is slapping a term policy and a whole life policy together and giving it a name. Old wine in new bottles.

One more thing to keep in mind. While it is nice to be loyal to whoever becomes your insurance agent—keep in mind that good service is worth a lot—it is also advisable to occasionally accept quotes from other agents or companies to see how their products stack up against what you have. Comparison shopping is a wise American tradition! For a few dollars' savings, it is usually best to remain with your old agency, but if the savings are substantial, it would be foolish not to purchase it. Just be certain you are comparing apples to apples and not to oranges. A new proposed policy may sound just like the old one, except for price, but may be vastly different. Give the former agent an opportunity to explain the differences, and, if you are still confused, seek out a third party for clarification. Beware of agents who rely heavily on replacing existing policies for their income! While not illegal, exactly, it is a highly unethical practice and can lead to loss of license for the agent. There are plenty of ethical agents around who truly want to serve you honestly, so don't traffic with someone who operates unethically.

Also, be aware that the premiums of many policies are loaded on the front end (especially whole life policies) to take care of administrative start-up and administrative costs. You start all over again with this with a new policy. And although the agent usually makes a renewal commission as long as the policy is in effect, it is a lesser amount than what is received during the initial period of the policy, usually the first year or whatever the initial renewal period is. It is sometimes in the agent's interest to replace policies, even within the company, although once again, an ethical agent won't operate that way. A good agent will take care of clients; this includes continually looking for the best policy that can be found for the money as time goes on in your relationship. This makes it unnecessary for you to go elsewhere—a situation in both your best interests.

Should you have problems with a policy or an agent or company, and can't obtain satisfaction, write or phone the insurance commissioner of your state. You can bet that will shake the tree! Don't bother the commissioner with truly petty problems, but if you have a serious area of dissension, that's the person to talk to. Many times, the state insurance commissioner's office has valuable educational information they are glad to supply those consumers who need it.

Forget the myth that some may hand you that they're "overinsured." This just isn't possible. Frankly, it's against the law. The insurance company that sells you the policy has to convince the commissioner that the beneficiary has this much legitimate financial interest in the insured, or the policy cannot be issued. You cannot, for example, insure anyone for ten million dollars if his or her loss isn't worth ten million (in cold, hard financial terms— we're obviously not speaking here of emotional worth!).

Another factor to consider in purchasing insurance is service. Both the service of the agent and of the company represented. Ask for the names of other clients (those who have filed claims) and solicit their opinion. In the case of insurances such as health insurance, ask the business offices of local physicians and hospitals if the company you are considering is rated as a "good pay" company. That is, do they pay promptly and in a businesslike fashion, or do they drag their feet, sometimes for months, perhaps contesting every claim. If you hook up with an insurance company like that, you may get a rude surprise when you first present your card at the health institution or office and it is refused! This rarely happens, but it does happen.

We all grumble at the insurance premiums we have to pay to

Don't wait for a crisis to realize how important good service is!

remain secure in our investment, but those premiums are cheap if a need to exercise the policy arises! It is a part of business life we cannot eliminate, and if you understand how insurance works, it's a darned good deal! All you are doing is spreading your own individual risk among a whole bunch of people. That way, in the event of a catastrophe (and they don't always happen to the "other guy"), your loss is manageable and your business can recover and survive.

One final factor to keep in mind. Where there are deductibles involved, such as in health insurances, it is best to take the highest deductible you can afford and spend the money on a high level of coverage at the upper end. If you have a choice between a policy with a $250 deductible and a $250,000 major medical limit, and one with a $500 deductible and a $500,000 major medical limit, choose the latter. Better yet, take the one with a $1,000 deductible and $1 million dollar in major medical limit. Almost anyone, even though it hurts, can come up with the $1,000 deductible, but the way hospital costs are rising even a million can get eaten up quickly in any long-term illness.

Most of us pay attention to the premium and not to what the premium actually buys. Do it the other way. Determine what your true requirements are and provide for that, adding more when you can afford it for true peace of mind. The method of premium payment you choose can also represent substantial savings. The most costly is paying monthly; the cheapest is to pay an "annualized premium" which is the year's total premium at a greatly reduced cost. Some life policies can be purchased with a one-time payment. If you can afford this kind of outlay, check first with your accountant to see if it really makes sense. Even though the savings may be substantial, it may not be as great as it appears, once you consider what the amount saved would bring when invested in a different instrument over the same period of time.

There are other kinds of insurance available, such as decreasing term, in which the premiums are lower than straight term due to the face value of the policy decreasing over the period of the policy to protect someone or something that decreases in (monetary) value. Increasing term works in just the opposite manner, raising the face value at regular intervals, such as every five years. Its purpose is to protect something that appreciates in value.

These, then, are the basic insurances needed in most salons. Your own situation may require others not mentioned here, but if you have taken the trouble to locate a competent insurance agent, he or she will keep you informed as your needs arise.

CHAPTER SIXTEEN

Marketing Your Business

Advertising doesn't work for me!

How many times have you heard someone say that, perhaps even yourself—usually right after you've run a $200 newspaper ad that brought in a grand total of three new customers!

The truth of the matter is that advertising per se often *doesn't* work. Kim and Sunny Baker, in their book *How to Promote, Publicize, and Advertise Your Growing Business*, John Wiley & Sons, Inc., estimate that "typical companies misspend fifty cents or more of every communication dollar for one reason or another." And they are talking about larger companies that employ professional agencies, not the typical salon owner who doesn't have the luxury of being able to afford professional advertising help.

The common mistakes, according to the Bakers, are "letting agencies do the thinking and make the choices for them, because they create communications without a clear message, because they use the wrong media, and because they don't know the difference between substantive changes and costly ones." They also misspend because "unscrupulous vendors take advantage of their lack of production knowledge." These are some of the reasons advertising quite often gives back poor returns, according to the authors, but there are many more.

To obtain maximum results from your advertising dollar, the first thing an owner should do is to begin thinking of the process as **marketing**, advertising being just one of the tools of that effort. Marketing your services and products is merely communicating to potential customers the benefits and advantages (for them) of what you offer for sale.

Remaining within the scope of this book, we can only deal here with the proper and systematic allocation of marketing and advertising dollars within the salon budget. This chapter deals only with proper budget allocations for advertising and marketing, and will identify the major concepts of marketing and advertising, but a more in-depth understanding requires additional study. Besides the aforementioned Baker book, we can highly recommend Jay Conrad Levinson's *Guerrilla Marketing, Guerrilla Marketing Attack, Guerrilla Marketing Weapons,* and *Guerrilla Marketing Excellence,* published by Houghton Mifflin. All of these books can be ordered from your local bookstore, should they not be in stock. Any of these publications will also refer you to other valuable resources, should you desire to broaden your knowledge.

A much more comprehensive concept than mere advertising, **marketing communications** include almost every form of communication your salon presents to the marketplace. There are four ingredients that marketing is based on: Product, Price, Place, and Promotion. Your targeted market will identify in which order these should be prioritized in your advertising efforts.

To maximize the effectiveness of your advertising dollar, it is prudent to allocate a set percentage of revenues in the annual budget. It is a standing rule of thumb that an advertising budget should approximate 3% of sales. Your goal is to determine how your advertising dollars should be spent, from among the many media available, including newspaper, radio, flyers, demonstrations, magazines, infomercials, and television, as well as many others. Including this in your budget in this manner makes it a fixed cost and results in more efficient planning of the dispersal of advertising dollars. When marketing is treated with the same respect as rent or utilities, it almost always is significantly more successful.

Be sure to include *all* forms of marketing and advertising communications you plan to utilize, including not only common media such as newspaper, radio, TV and outdoor ads, but newsletters, mailings, flyers, publicity releases, Yellow Pages and other directory ads, special promotions, business cards and letterhead, in-salon signage, T-shirts or other promotional clothing, specialty items, and anything else that clients or potential clients will see, receive, or be exposed to. Anything that perceptually promotes your image is advertising.

The advertising or marketing budget should consist of two basic parts, **directed funds** and **discretionary funds**. Directed funds are those monies targeted at planned advertising and marketing activities, while discretionary funds are those set aside for unexpected marketing and advertising opportunities. The portion of discretionary funds may vary, but should be in a lesser proportion than directed funds, usually on a 4:1 or a one-fifth basis. For instance, if your monthly advertising budget is $500, $400 should be in previously planned directed funds and $100 in discretionary funds. Discretionary funds would be profitably kept in an interest-bearing account, even a savings account that allows speedy withdrawal without penalty. The $100 should be spent only if a bona fide advertising opportunity presents itself that, in your best judgment, will allow a profitable return on the investment.

Don't spend it just because it's there. After a reasonable period of time, say six months, if you haven't utilized a significant portion of the discretionary funds, it is time to reevaluate your budget, and perhaps allocate a higher percentage to the directed funds portion. You might do well to build the discretionary funds account to a predetermined figure, say a thousand dollars and maintain it there until used, redirecting future such funds into the directed funds portion and increasing the frequency or size of the media used there. Or, you can experiment with different forms of marketing.

It is important that you preplan the majority of your marketing expenditures around the goals you wish to reach. This serves several purposes. First, whenever you plan something, you give it more thought and attention than you would to last-minute decisions. This, by itself, makes your decisions wiser. Second, planning ahead lets you avoid missing golden opportunities. Third, preplanning an annual budget can lead to significant savings and better use of your dollars.

Also, referring to the experience presented at the beginning of this chapter, where you have spent $200 for a newspaper ad which brought in three new clients...think about this: If you retain each of those clients and the average client in your salon spends $154 per year, then was it a waste? Add to that the fact that each new client, if cultivated properly, should send in an average of three referrals each, and they in turn send in referrals. It becomes evi-

Assess advertising results as accurately as possible.

dent that this particular investment wasn't as bad as you may have thought. In reality, it may have been a very profitable use of advertising dollars!

In general, and particularly when first implementing an advertising and/or marketing program, it is advisable to "track" the success of each effort. For instance, if you spent $1,000 on a newspaper ad campaign, and you have determined that it brought in 25 new service clients, and you spent another $1,000 on a series of radio ads that you estimate resulted in 20 new customers, you can begin to compare apples to apples and see where your advertising budget should be spent for maximum return.

Keep in mind, however, that money spent in advertising is not always judged solely on its immediate impact. Perhaps one of the avenues you utilize (say, a TV ad for example) doesn't return the same number of new clients per dollar as does your billboard out on Highway 218 in the short-term analysis, but over a period of time it increases market awareness and respect, not only among new clients but present ones. That is a definite value as well. This is sometimes hard to determine, but if you notice clients regularly mentioning that television spot (in our scenario), you have some idea that it is being effective. If virtually no one says they have seen it, then you know that the ad was probably not very effective.

Whatever the media, there should be a definite increase in sales from the use of your advertising dollars. Clients should be asked if they have seen your ads, or, if new clientele is received, you should be asking how they chose your salon. By quizzing your client base, you will know the best forms and amount to advertise.

Perhaps the very best form of advertising for salons is referrals, so you might consider some form of renumeration for those clients who send you new business. This can and should be done in a manner that is tax deductible.

CHAPTER SEVENTEEN

Plan for Prosperity

There are many uses for your prosperity dollars, but the most important use most times is to pay off existing debts.

Debt creates costs through interest on borrowed monies, a definite outflow. Monies should be set aside for equipment replacement or upgrades. You may be thinking of alternative sites or additional locations. Remember, too, that this money does not have to stay in the company. It can be withdrawn for personal uses and here the sky is the limit.

As prosperity comes your way, you will probably discover that your outflow seems to equal your inflow. There is never enough! As your disposable income increases, you will look back and say, "How could we have made it on the money we were making before?" Therefore, you need to again plan for prosperity. Develop a short-term five-year plan and a longer, ten-year plan. Base it on questions such as—*What do you want to do? Where do you want to be?* Begin to put price tags on these goals and then save to achieve.

As conditions change rapidly, it would be ill advised to recommend investment vehicles for prosperity dollars in this forum. That is a job for you and your accountant and perhaps an investment counselor to work on, within the economic situation of the moment.

At the close of each business year, you should sit down with your accountant and plan for the future. First, review your mission statement to be certain you are on track with your stated goals and philosophy. Perhaps these have changed and if so, they need to be incorporated, and a plan implemented to help achieve all your goals, short- and long-term.

You need to review your business plan and develop the plan for the coming year, providing for a new annual budget to achieve the profit levels you have set as your goal.

Once you are satisfied with the direction you intend to take and have a plan in place to reach your goals, have a meeting with your staff, explaining where the salon is and where it is headed, how they are included, what you expect from them, and what they can expect from you. Solicit their input as well, as they may come up with means of achieving your goals that you might not have thought of or considered. Including staff members in this process is also the best way of making sure they will work hard to reach those goals, especially when they realize that your goals will benefit them as well.

Planning for prosperity means learning how to spot trends and capitalizing on them. Even though we are predominantly smaller businesses, major national and international trends impact upon our business, and those salon owners that recognize

and take advantage of them will profit the most. Texts such as *Megatrends* by John Naisbitt, and *The Age Wave* by Ken Dychtwald, Ph.D, along with other, current, knowledgeable forecasters, are invaluable for obtaining such information.

Monitor trade magazines for their forecasts. They are usually knowledgeable about the future and with their resources many times are able to spot indicators of future trends in the salon business. Read and absorb what new trade books have to say.

Index

Notes

Notes

Notes

Notes

Notes

Notes

Notes

Notes

Notes

Notes

Notes

Notes

Notes

Notes

Notes

Notes

Notes

Notes